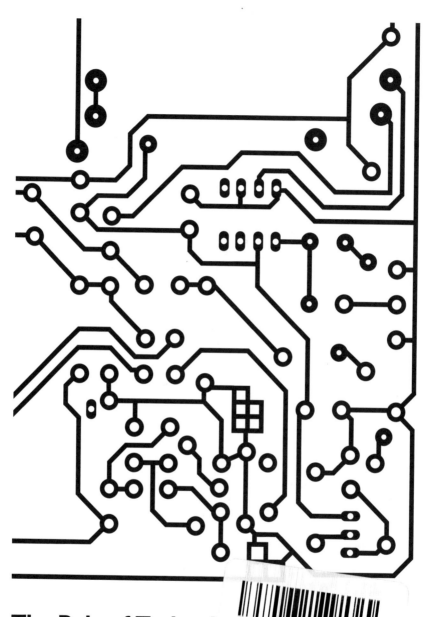

The Role of Technology in Tomorrow's Schools

ISBN 0-89056-028-5

Printed in the United States of America
10 9 8 7 6 5 4 3 2 1

⬤ ⬤ ⬤ Contents

◐ ◐ ◐ Foreword

In October 2007, the Evaluation Systems group of Pearson gathered educators and policy makers at a conference in Chicago to discuss the role of technology in the schools of tomorrow. Stemming from their various backgrounds—superintendents, board of education members, teachers—conference participants presented a vision for how various players—students, teachers, school systems, credentialing agencies—might use technology to streamline processes and to better prepare students to face the challenges of the global economy.

Following is a brief summary of each of the conference participants' presentations.

James E. Barker warns that technology is vital for preparing students to be able to navigate and compete on the boundless global world stage.

Larry Rosenstock discusses the importance of broadening our technical schools to provide our students with a complete academic background as well as a broad understanding and knowledge of industry in order to prepare them for careers focused on global cooperation. He also discusses some of the practical applications of technology at High Tech High.

Jennifer L. Husbands focuses on how quality teachers are hired and trained at High Tech High, stressing that these teachers are not trained to use technology but to give students the opportunity to use technology themselves to showcase their learning.

Yong Zhao shows us how computers and teachers should be thought of as equal sources of learning and education, with each assigned specific tasks. He describes various applications of virtual reality existing throughout the world today, and stresses the importance of preparing our children to thrive in a digital environment.

While Jason Kamras admits that there are many things technology can do in the classroom to make a teacher's job easier, he believes that preparing, training, and maintaining high-quality teachers is what will prepare students for the future, and that our approach so far has been "woefully inadequate."

In response to what she feels has been an avoidance in the 2008 presidential election of any real discussion of using technology in the schools of tomorrow to create 24/7 learning communities, Penelope M. Earley offers an open letter to the future president of the United States, outlining several points with which to begin these discussions.

Tom Welch emphasizes that in order for educators to make the most of the new technologies available to them, they must first move from the idea of education focused around the school to education focused on learning itself, with the idea that learning should have no limits in terms of time and place, instead taking place twenty-four hours a day, seven days a week, and across seven continents, and that students at different levels should be able to move ahead or take more time, as needed.

Sue Gee discusses the importance of remaining flexible in terms of both how we prepare our teachers and how we design our technological infrastructure.

Richard Paula discusses the initiatives of the Quabbin Regional School District and its desire to move toward integrating information and engaging students in the process of learning.

William Thomas details the origins of the Southern Regional Education Board, describing its recent focus on online learning through the creation of state virtual schools.

Ronald A. Berk explores technology through the idea of using music in the classroom to enhance learning, citing both theoretical and research evidence related to how music affects the brain; describing technological tools for successfully bringing music into the classroom; and suggesting practical ways to select appropriate music and incorporate it into learning.

Tracy Loken Weber focuses on the importance of technology for motivating adult learners and discusses the role it should play in adult basic education, general educational development, English as a Second Language, and workforce development.

Jamey Fitzpatrick discusses the value of online learning through the context of Michigan Virtual University, but warns that it is not a one-size-fits-all solution, and that we need to invest in training our teachers to use online technologies so they can become effective online teachers.

Sandy Kress looks at technology in terms of federal legislation, insisting that we need to tie technology to key objectives of education law and policy in order to fully benefit from its power—that is, both to expand the learning environment from its current "either/or" environment and to be able to gather and interpret information about where students are in terms of strengths and weaknesses.

Dee Hopkins discusses the inadequacies of the public high school system and its inability to adequately prepare students to succeed in the global age. Rising to the challenge, Texas has been active in addressing this problem by developing a college-ready default curriculum; revising its state assessments; and investing in the Texas High School Project—a partnership dedicated to increasing the number of graduates prepared for college success, whose giant step in this direction was the creation of University Preparatory High School.

John E. Jacobson describes the characteristics of today's generation of teacher candidates, making the point that traditional face-to-face methods of learning are not enough to engage them in learning. He discusses the value of online learning and its development over the last several years at Stephen F. Austin State University.

Glenn Thomas makes the connection between student learning, technology, and global sustainability through the context of the Millennium Project's report on what will be needed in the year 2030 in terms of technologies and learning support.

Rick Eiserman changes the focus to look at how technology can best be used to capture data on teacher preparation and certification and use that data to measure school improvement and student achievement, citing the Georgia Professional Standards Commission as a successful model.

Dale Janssen reports on California's commitment to quality data collection, outlining its many initiatives and discussing where each is in the process.

W. Robert Houston reiterates that the realm of education has yet to realize the full potential of technology, falling further behind as the speed at which innovations occur rapidly increases. In order to make the kind of changes that technology will allow and begin educating differently, we need to first accept the validity of the innovations themselves.

The conference provided a variety of perspectives on the role that technology can and should play in the future of education—in learning, data collection, teacher preparation, and elsewhere. Although many of these ideas have been put into practice, it is clear that much more work needs to be done—in terms of both implementing procedures and convincing those resistant to change—to make the most of the technology currently available as well as the innovations to come.

For most of the papers, the informal tone of the speaker's presentation has been retained. Evaluation Systems wishes to acknowledge that all of the papers in this book represent a significant commitment of time and effort on the part of the authors to prepare and present this information at the 2007 conference, and later to prepare the papers for publication. Evaluation Systems thanks all the contributors to this book. The views expressed herein are those of the authors and do not necessarily represent the positions of the Evaluation Systems group of Pearson.

Evaluation Systems
Pearson
P.O. Box 226
Amherst, Massachusetts 01004-0226
(412) 256-0444

www.nesinc.com

www.pearsonschool.com

O O O Using Technology in Schools to Embrace Global Opportunities

James E. Barker

Education is big business, and it needs to operate like a business designed to improve a student's future. Only then can we accomplish our goal of preparing the world's best and brightest to compete in the new flat world. A world-class education is the engine of the global economy; those who have it, win; those who do not, lose. Over a number of years, I've had the good fortune to work with many international businesspeople. We have about seven countries that we deal with on a regular basis, including our sister city in China and our programs with Poland and Germany.

With the Internet, education and companies are only a click away. The Internet has created a connected global community. Through the pairing of exchanges with technology in our classrooms, the district is becoming a place of global opportunity. For many students, the classroom is a portal to a world of possibilities. Every day, education and business are interfacing on everything from astrophysics to zoology, using a tool that is free to those who have access, knowledge, and opportunity.

For example, a free global conference is currently taking place on the Web, which involves approximately sixty-two countries worldwide. In this format, all anyone needs to do is go online, and he or she can interface, interact, and have dialogues with educators from all over the world. This is truly the free market of intellectual capital. Concurrently, students are setting up their own pages—similar to MySpace pages—to post any number of issues regarding trigonometry, writing, and other areas of study. So, from a technology perspective, if you have Internet capability, knowledge, and access, you can forever change a student's ability to participate and compete in the new knowledge economy. Access is being expanded worldwide to this new frontier. Corporations and universities are also reaching out to underserved countries to accelerate their participation in this new economy. In fact, MIT's computer lab just received a huge corporate grant, with which they're going to send out 100–120 million computers to underserved countries without electricity.

Dr. James E. Barker is a member of the Pennsylvania State Board of Education and Superintendent of the School District, City of Erie, Pennsylvania.

These computers have a crank on the side, and every crank will afford 15 minutes of Internet access. The world is shrinking, and our classrooms need to connect with others beyond their community, their state, and their country. A successful classroom today must link to the global community. It is our ongoing challenge to access and utilize the world's resources to help each and every student.

I had the good fortune to go to India with an executive from a global corporation, who said, "Everybody's talking about high tech. Come with me; I want to show you something." So at about seven-thirty in the morning we went out to a field that had a mowed area about six inches high, surrounded by tall weeds. I was wondering what he could possibly have in mind when he said, "I want to show you where the great technology leaders are coming from." About ten minutes later, as if on cue, a group of young people began to arrive and kneeled on this field of grass, awaiting their teacher. There are no boundaries for those who want to learn using technology. It is clear that many countries understand and have promoted the benefits of a high-tech education to their students.

Part of our challenge is educating American students about their counterparts around the world who are hungry for knowledge and eager to learn. And that's one of the reasons educators need to be informed that jobs are the prize for well-educated youth in this competitive arena of worldwide connectivity. Every teacher needs to prepare world-class learners for the global economy. As that corporate executive stated, "This is where it begins—with the motivation of students coming and kneeling in a field and waiting for their teacher to arrive." Pair this with global opportunities and technology, and the old work barriers of time and place are removed.

For instance, many companies are doing their accounting, payroll, tech support, and other functions over the Internet in countries like India. The jobs go where students/workers have been educated for these technology-based solutions. The fact is, students in China, India, and other parts of the world are using technology to change what it means to work. The skill sets and knowledge are no longer the purview of geography or controlled by a country. The reward for the globally prepared workforce within this new knowledge-working group is a better standard of living—a nicer home, a new automobile, and more expendable income. Businesses assessing this workforce are moving individuals from poverty to possibility. Students in many countries are willing to invest whatever time or energy is necessary in becoming world-class learners in their respective fields. The challenge for educators is to create engaging learning experiences that motivate American students to consistently compete on this competitive world stage. One way to accomplish this is by using contemporary technology to access information worldwide to help students more fully realize their potential as citizens of the world. The old text-and-teacher model only reflects good teaching in a Norman Rockwell painting.

A new dawn is upon educators. The future will belong to those who can navigate and compete in this new boundless, global knowledge economy. The best hope is in using technology to access the world to redefine and redesign this experience called education.

O O O What is the "High Tech" in High Tech High?

Larry Rosenstock

Albert Einstein said, "Overemphasis on competition and premature specialization on the grounds of obedient usefulness killed the spirit upon which all cultural life depends, specialized knowledge included."

As I believe Einstein would have wholeheartedly agreed with, we should focus less on global competition and more on global cooperation. We should avoid narrow skills training in our high schools because the average high school student today will have eight to ten jobs in a lifetime. Thus, our occupational/technical programs must focus less on occupational specificity and more on broad understanding and knowledge of industries.

Broadening the Scope of Technical Schools

I taught carpentry in Massachusetts after law school, and it was formative for me because it opened my eyes to the divisions in our schools. Under the Boston desegregation plan, there were kids going to school with kids who didn't look like them, and it was the first time they were doing so. I realized in the first few days that the working-class students in my classroom were every bit as bright as the middle-class kids I had just gone to law school with. When I later became a principal of a 350-year-old public high school, I was still unable to get working-class kids next to middle-class kids in classes. We were thwarted by a very few white middle-class parents who felt—wrongly—that the treatment their children received would be made worthless if we provided the same treatment for everybody. Our public schools are now more segregated than they were in 1953, before *Brown v. Board of Education.*

Common planning time for technical and academic teachers is an exception in our country's schools. We are laboring under an old model, in which technical skills and academics are divided, and it's very tough to change. Bruce Alberts, former president of the National Academy of Sciences, shows a great slide of a school district. The slide shows multiple vectors: state standards, standardized tests, textbooks, parent

Larry Rosenstock is CEO at High Tech High in San Diego, California, a public charter school management organization developed in concert with San Diego's high tech industry.

associations, school boards, teachers' unions, everything. As a former chemist, he then points out that this is what is known in chemistry as a system in perfect equilibrium, and that systems in perfect equilibrium are very hard to change.

The name High Tech High is a bit of a misnomer. Tom Vander Ark, former executive director for education at the Bill and Melinda Gates Foundation, said "High Tech High is really a great liberal arts school in disguise" (Jacobs 2003). A key difference about us, however, is that we have created a school that has no "ability grouping"—which, in truth, is actually based on experience rather than ability. We have no "tracking" whatsoever—our students are accepted through a blind, zip-code-based lottery. We know nothing about their grades, race, special needs; they are randomly selected using an algorithm that only has their name, grade, and zip code. One hundred percent of our graduates have gotten into college, 70 percent of whom are going to four-year colleges. Fifty percent of our graduates are first-generation college students.

Practical Applications

Our students produce some really amazing things. They publish books and make documentary films; they build robots, submersibles, and hovercraft. Our junior class has published five books, including two books about San Diego Bay. The latest—*San Diego Bay: A Story of Exploitation and Restoration*—was entirely done by students and contains an introduction by Jane Goodall, who also wrote the introduction to last year's *Perspectives of San Diego Bay: A Field Guide*.

An innovative project done by our seniors last spring was dubbed Analog Flash for Windows—"analog" because most are mechanical, not digital; "flash" because they're interactive; and "windows" because that's where they fit (our windows are 24" x 24" x 5"). We had made a decision a while back that the projects students do, like the books they produce, ought to have lasting value. But at the end of the school year two years ago, many student projects ended up in a big Dumpster outside the school—creating an environmentally unsound situation as well. Since then we have doubled our efforts in this area, putting our focus into calling for projects of lasting value. Three teachers collaborated on this particular project—an artist, a physicist, and an engineer. These teachers wanted to create installations that other students could benefit from and that would establish a permanent "artifactorium" in the school. First they and the students involved visited San Francisco's Exploratorium to see how an interactive science museum sets up its projects. Next they went to the de Young Museum to study methods of curation, realizing that the goal was to show physics concepts as art. They also consulted *The Way*

Things Work—an amazing book by David Macaulay—for inspiration, and studied the work of artist Christo in order to help students plan their projects. Then they did a few mock-ups, experimenting with different types of designs and models.

Thus, Analog Flash for Windows was born. Fifty seniors worked in pairs to create twenty-five projects, with the goal of either creating art about physics and engineering, or using physics and engineering to create art. These interactive installations are amazing, and inspire visits from children and adults of all ages. Usually the physics and calculus that underlie each creation are written next to the piece to provide a deeper understanding of the project.

The physics exam tied to Analog Flash for Windows is indeed rigorous, yet it is closely related to the projects themselves. The purpose of this particular exam has to do with understanding how these curated installations really work. There are twenty-five pairs of students, and in order to pass the exam, each pair needs to teach the physics of their project to the other twenty-four teams, and in turn needs to learn the physics of each of the other twenty-four projects. Having students teach and learn from each other in this way produces a multiplier effect. And thus we return to Einstein's point, calling for an emphasis on collaboration rather than competition.

Reference

Jacobs, G. 2003. High Tech High providing new take on education: Charter school's goal to meld public, private partnership. *San Diego Business Journal*, February 3.

⬤ ⬤ ⬤ Teacher Preparation and Ongoing Professional Development at High Tech High

Jennifer L. Husbands

Teachers come to High Tech High in a variety of ways. Our current teachers and other colleagues are probably our richest source of teacher referral. We network with regional universities, as well as participate in local and national job fairs. We also do a bit of advertising, both with Carney, Sandoe and Associates—mostly an independent school placement organization—and with Craig's List, and have gotten some wonderful teachers that way. We also love to pull prospective private school teachers into the public school sector, and have a number of teachers among us for whom that's been the case.

The Hiring Process

To apply, prospective teachers submit their résumé and cover letter online. Following our review, we may choose to conduct a brief interview by phone. Candidates who pass the paper and phone screens are invited to campus for a full day interview. Many times these take the form of what we call our hiring bonanza, in which anywhere from ten to twenty-five teacher candidates come to campus—typically on a Friday—and we interview them as a group. During the day candidates will teach a sample lesson and interview with both teachers and students. The student-candidate interview is very important. Students instinctively know who they can and cannot learn from, and so we take their feedback very seriously when making our hiring decisions. Candidates also informally interact with other staff and students throughout the day. At the end of the day, the teachers and students who participated in the interviews will come together to debrief on each of the candidates, and candidates who score highly will be made offers to teach at a High Tech High school.

What kinds of people do we make offers to? We hire a diverse cross-section of individuals to teach in our schools. They might be career changers or people fresh out of undergraduate school. They might be

Jennifer L. Husbands, Ph.D., is Director of Teacher Credentialing and Support for High Tech High, a charter school development organization in San Diego, California, where she leads the nation's first charter-school based teacher certification program.

people who have taught in other settings, such as private schools, community colleges, or outdoor education centers. At High Tech High, we're able to hire without regard to credential status. Because we have an in-house alternative certification program, we can hire whomever we feel is most qualified for a position and work with him or her toward earning a credential.

The Teacher Intern Program

Our Teacher Intern Program was approved by the California Commission on Teacher Credentialing in August 2004, making us the first charter-school-based teacher certification program in California—and possibly the nation. The program was developed in response to some policy changes at the state and federal levels. Initially, charter-school teachers in California did not need teaching credentials, but that law was changed right around the time we opened our first school, so we responded to that change. The two-year program is tuition-free to participants, and our classes are offered on-site. The program represents a partnership with the University of San Diego, a few of whose staff members do some of the teaching, but the majority of our courses are taught by our in-house teachers and administrators.

While our program prepares teachers to succeed in any California school, as it earns them a California teaching credential, the program is context driven, emphasizing our project-based learning pedagogy and the differentiation of instruction in our diverse classrooms. Since we are a public school organization, we're not immune to the highly qualified teacher requirements of No Child Left Behind. Our interns must have a BA or BS at minimum, although many have master's degrees and a few have PhDs. Eligible interns need to demonstrate their subject-matter competence, which they do through their undergraduate or graduate degrees or by taking state-approved tests. The highly qualified requirements present a challenge for us, as many of our teachers teach two core subject areas, which is one of our strategies for keeping the number of students each teacher sees each day to a minimum. Therefore, interns have to verify not one but two core subject areas for their highly qualified status. So while our compliance numbers continually rise, it's a challenge as we bring new teachers into the system. Although the intern credential is considered a valid document for No Child Left Behind purposes, there has recently been a lawsuit filed against the U.S. Department of Education questioning whether or not the credential is sufficient to meet the highly qualified provisions in NCLB. We'll be watching this case very closely to see what happens.

Right now our intern teachers must be at least half-time teachers of record in the classroom, so we need to feel confident that they're ready for that assignment. We receive numerous inquiries from individuals who want a more traditionally structured student/teacher based program of preparation. In order to expand our teacher credentialing to meet that need, we established a post-secondary institution, which, once accredited, will house our certification programs. In the meantime, we've launched our own graduate school, with an approved Master of Education program in teacher leadership; and in the fall of 2008 we'll launch our school leadership program. We've already begun the process of securing accreditation from our regional accrediting body. This new institution—a graduate school of education embedded in a K–12 charter organization—may be the first of its kind.

Foundations of Learning at High Tech High

When we talk about our work in adult education—both the credentialing programs and the master's programs—we describe them as "leading with practice and infusing with theory." Following are the design principles that undergird the practice within our schools, as well as the theoretical framework that guides our work in adult learning.

I'll start with the three High Tech High design principles. The first is personalization, by which we mean that all students are known well by at least one adult. The second, common intellectual mission, refers to the fact that we do not track our students. Every one of them is working toward a college prep curriculum, they're all taking the same core courses, and they're not ability grouped. The third is adult-world connection, which stresses the importance of students seeing a connection between the work they do in their classrooms and the real world—the world of work—outside. To make the connection between the two as transparent as possible, we bring people from the world of work into our schools when we can.

In terms of our adult learning, we follow the four features of an effective learning environment set out by Bransford and colleagues in *How People Learn* (2000): (1) learner centered, (2) knowledge centered, (3) assessment centered, and (4) community centered. A learner-centered environment is one that focuses on the particular needs of the learner, and what is being learned is applicable in that context. In a knowledge-centered environment, learning activities are organized around valuable content—things that, in our case, teachers feel are worth knowing. In an assessment-centered environment, learners know what is expected of them and how they'll be assessed, and that they'll be given multiple opportunities for revision and resubmission. A community-centered environment seeks to foster communities of learning, where it is safe to explore ideas and take intellectual risks. Through our adult education, we strive to foster collegial and congenial social environments to support learning.

Taken together, we hope that our practices with adult learners reflect our practices with students, and vice versa.

Technology in Practice

At High Tech High, training teachers to use technology is not our focus. We use technology primarily for two things: production and presentation. Production refers to student work, whether they're producing a documentary film or making a tool or other piece of equipment that actually works. Presentation refers to how and when our students demonstrate their learning. Students do presentations several times throughout the year and then as a gateway from one grade level to the next at the end of a year—we call this the transitional presentation of learning. And so they might use PowerPoint; they might display their digital portfolios; they might make a Web site. At High Tech High, we don't learn about technology as much as we make it available to students to showcase their learning.

Reference

Bransford, J. D., A. L. Brown, and R. R. Cocking, eds. 2000. *How people learn: Brain, mind, experience, and school.* Washington, DC: National Academy Press.

⬤ ⬤ ⬤ Never Send a Human to Do a Machine's Job: How Technology Should Be Used in Schools

Yong Zhao

In April, results of a study supported by Congress stated that technology does not make a difference in student test scores. After one year, this $10 million study—which compiled data on the effects on testing after supplying first, fourth, and sixth graders with computers and software—found that there was no significant difference in test scores between those who had used the software and those who hadn't. If you read the report carefully, however, it also states that although the software recommended that teachers be present, 8 percent of the classrooms were without teachers for that year. In light of this fact, my reading of the results takes a different turn: basically that computers are just as effective as teachers.

The State of Education in America

The United States is perhaps in one of its darkest ages in terms of education. Many Americans call the request to put another $43 billion into Iraq a big mistake. The truth is, the No Child Left Behind Act is an even bigger mistake for the country. Why? Because it's aimed at the wrong thing. As a country that has been at the center of innovation for so many years, we're suddenly looking to other countries as models for our education system, and yet China, India, Singapore—they all want to be like the United States. American education needs to be more American—not replicate what the others are doing. A National Center on Education and the Economy report clearly showed that even if our students had the same talents as Chinese or Indian students, Chinese and Indians earn seven times less (2006). All other things being equal, an employer would hire a Chinese or an Indian over an American. Our American education system has to produce people with different talents.

Dr. Yong Zhao is a University Distinguished Professor and the Director of the Center of Technology & Teaching at the College of Education at Michigan State University in East Lansing, Michigan.

When you look across the world at different educational systems, everybody—if they're not consumed with fighting a war—is in the process of serious reform. Personalization is the major theme in England's reform movement, while more flexibility is being touted in Japan, Hong Kong, and various other places. But U.S. education reform is perhaps the most backwards right now.

I think we have made several mistakes along the way in terms of educational technology. The first mistake was that it wasn't introduced as a particular solution to any problem. When computers were initially put into the schools, there was no legitimate problem to solve. The computers were introduced as a teacher's tool in an attempt to improve the teacher's presentation and general teaching skills at a time when most teachers—after so many years of teaching—could more than handle the traditional way of teaching. Even after 1995 almost every state introduced requirements mandating teachers to incorporate professional technology into their classrooms. Today we still don't see very many individual uses of technology. The most popular use of technology in many schools today is PowerPoint and SMART Boards. And these are mostly used by teachers, not students. So there's no qualitative change. For many schools computers have indeed become a problem rather than a solution. Schools spend as much money and effort blocking access to the Internet as they're spending building that access. The Confucius Institute offers online Chinese to high schools. When we try to contact the schools, we have a lot of problems dealing with their IP addresses and firewalls. We cannot get through; the kids cannot chat with our instructors.

The second mistake we made is thinking that classroom learning has to be led by a teacher. Schools are still being thought of in terms of classrooms—classrooms in which teachers still have the most power. Therefore, we let the teachers make the decisions about how to use technology, and leadership doesn't do anything about it. If you think about it, computers duplicate a lot of the teacher's functions. As a teacher, do you want to facilitate practice or do you want to present information? We need to differentiate these functions. When you have two species completely filling the same niche, they can kill each other.

Schools need to think about using computers to do what computers do best. As the congressional study showed, computers can do very well with offering practice—remedial, math fluency, and reading fluency. Then teachers can be left to do what they do best. Teachers represent human interaction and higher level thinking. The model we're using now with our online Chinese courses through Michigan State University has students working individually for four hours and teachers interacting with them for one hour. The interactions occur in very small groups—five students to one teacher—and the result is much better than the current classroom ratio of one language teacher to twenty-five students.

The third mistake was our failure to fully anticipate the transformation that has occurred. As adults, we have completely ignored what children do. There is a very popular Web site in China called iapartment. The idea is very simple: you get online and you can rent a virtual apartment and date virtually. Then you can virtually marry in front of a virtual priest and basically start living your virtual life. Not only can you buy furniture and decorate your rooms but you can have virtual arguments with your virtual spouse over the virtual color of your virtual tub. Psychologically the process is very similar to having real interactions.

The Virtual Future

This is really a multimedia, 3-D socialization environment. Singapore's ministry of education runs a virtual professional development program for school leaders. While this is fascinating, what's more interesting is the virtual economy, in which many people are actually making money. One Chinese woman immigrated to Germany without a job. Once in Germany, she bought some virtual land in Second Life—a 3-D virtual world. She started developing it into virtual rental gardens, people started buying them, and she became the first person to make a million dollars selling virtual properties. Now I wouldn't recommend quitting your day job, but these things are definitely possible. This virtual economy is very fascinating. It's really no different from owning something tangible as far as commerce goes. A virtual space station recently sold for $25,000. The guy who bought it wants to develop it into a virtual nightclub. These things are happening.

Gold farming refers to role-playing games in which players acquire valuable items by carrying out particular actions within a game. Basically there are hundreds of thousands of people from different countries— China, Romania, the United States—playing the games and selling the points, and those people are called gold farmers. And then people set up industries—across the border in Mexico, in China, in Romania—called virtual sweatshops. So there's a huge economy going on, and this economy is not really virtual—it's connected with the real economy, a feasible economy. This is going on now and so will be a big part of our future. Virtual is part of the transformation technology has made in our society. Look at YouTube—it's amazing how such a young company could play such a major role in our presidential campaign. But the point of YouTube—podcasting, wikis, blogs—is that everybody, as Rupert Murdoch said, can become an author, expressing his or her ideas through multimedia. There is amazing potential in this; if you do podcasts or get on YouTube, you can have access to more people than Fox News. We need to prepare our students to make use of this new technology to express their ideas and talents, which are normally suppressed during the school day because of the emphasis on mathematical, logical, and verbal skills.

At the same time, technology transformation made this new environment a dangerous place. A few years ago, an eighteen-year-old German boy celebrated his birthday by creating a super computer virus. Within twenty-four hours—boom! Today there are cyberwars going on. Countries employ hackers to attack each other; Estonia and Russia recently had a war, China and Taiwan, China and the United States—all of this is going on. When you destroy someone's e-mail in-box, is it the same as throwing a rock through someone's window? Does it feel the same? Why do people feel less guilty when they copy, cut, and paste text into their writing rather than copying from a real book? We need to understand the physicality and the psychology of this. As adults, as educators, are we understanding this transformation?

Using the Power of Technology

As education leaders, we need to rethink schools as organizations that provide learning opportunities—not as classrooms. We need to think about computers and teachers as equal sources of learning and education, and differentiate their functions and assign them different tasks. This is a very important component, but it's also very hard to accept. We have always been apologetic in saying that computers are never going to replace teachers. True, they're not going to replace human beings, but we can let them fulfill a function. They should not be controlled by one individual who may or may not like them. We have invested so much, there is so much power—we need to unleash it.

A basic rule is to not let teachers do things that they do not want to do or that they cannot do as effectively as—or as inexpensively as—technology can. The first example of this involves personal response systems, which use very simple technology. In universities and schools, one of our biggest problems is trying to gauge where students are. With this little piece of relatively inexpensive technology you can know right away what's happening in the classroom in terms of learning. The second thing is a design for a series of language learning programs. China used to have one teacher per seventy-five students in a college English class, which is not an effective ratio. With computers you can design a model in which students spend enough computer time to complete one unit, after which they have a meeting with a teacher and a small group of students. In this way, you separate the functions of the systems. The Chinese minister of education has mandated that all universities implement this design into their language program. The general idea here is to make computers do what they do best. If you learn a foreign language, you want to practice pronunciation, grammar; this can be accomplished much more efficiently by computers than by teachers.

In the United States, everybody wants to learn Chinese, but either there are no teachers in this country to meet those demands, or schools are not free to hire a Chinese teacher for political reasons. But with online learning, there's no reason we cannot offer Chinese, Spanish, or even Arabic to every child who wants to learn it. In fact, we currently have a lot of systems available at the Confucius Institute.

We have to accept the re-adaptation of computers. Winston Churchill said "We shape our buildings; thereafter they shape us." We cannot resist the idea; we must accept the virtual environment we are in now and therefore start the conversation about digital citizenship.

Preparing Our Students for the Future

Why do we have to accept the transformation? Because we need to educate our children to live in this digital virtual environment, to be smart consumers, to be good citizens, and to be community leaders in the digital age. Leading a digital virtual community takes very different skills than leading a physical community. We need to teach children how to make a living in a digital environment. To be successful in this environment, you need the skills to organize forty or fifty people from all walks of life and convince them not only to follow your command but to let you take all the spoils. This is all very challenging, and our young people need to be prepared.

Most product development today is spread across many countries. Telecommuting has allowed people to work together in this new global environment. Ten years ago, when I was a graduate student at the University of Illinois, I thought we had reached the end of innovation. I couldn't imagine anything new being needed because we already had all of the cool stuff. And then, what happened? Google, YouTube, MySpace, Facebook. We have to teach our children to become innovators and entrepreneurs—not just consumers.

When we talk about technology, we have to first accept that technology can do certain functions more efficiently than teachers. And this initiative has to be led by school leaders to help staff rethink how their schools connect. When we think about global forces, we need to think about our unique niche, prepare our unique talents—not compete in the same domain as others.

And finally, we have to teach digital citizenship in the United States. None of the states in the United States has even dealt with this issue, instead focusing on technology standards, such as how to hold a mouse. If we are to embark on exploring technology to prepare our children to compete, they need to learn how to be respectful and savvy users of that technology.

Reference

National Center on Education and the Economy, 2006. *Tough choices or tough times: The report of the New Commission on the skills of the American workforce.* San Francisco: Jossey-Bass.

⬤ ⬤ ⬤ It's All About People

Jason Kamras

What I have found over the last decade is that we, in the education world, love to talk about the promise of technology but sometimes forget the underlying importance of the people who stand in front of our children every day: the teachers. The truth is that all the computers, interactive whiteboards, digital assessment tools, and Web-based curricula in the world won't take us where we need to go without high-quality teachers.

My focus here, then, is not on the educational uses of technology but on why I believe our public education system's entire approach to human capital—from preparation to professional development to evaluation and compensation—is fundamentally broken.

Preparation

Many teacher preparation programs in this country simply do not prepare their students to serve as effective educators. A recent study by the National Council on Teacher Quality, for example, revealed that very few schools of education actually teach their students about the science of reading instruction (2006). In fact, nearly all the schools studied received a failing grade in this important area.

On-the-Job Professional Development

Most teacher professional development in America amounts to a series of half-day workshops that are largely irrelevant to what is actually happening in classrooms. If we're serious about educating our children, then we need a new, robust commitment to professional development. We need master teachers to provide job-embedded training to their peers over the course of months, not days. It's incredibly difficult to change adult behavior, and nowhere is this truer than in education. Real change requires a real commitment.

Jason Kamras was the 2005 National Teacher of the Year and currently serves as the Director of Human Capital Strategy for Teachers in the District of Columbia Public Schools (DCPS).

Evaluation and Compensation

We don't adequately evaluate teachers in this country, and as a result, we allow too many ineffective educators to remain in the classroom. In addition, our teacher compensation systems rarely offer incentives for high-performing individuals to serve in the schools that need them the most; to stay in those schools; and to teach critical shortage subjects such as math, science, and special education.

A Model of Excellence

High Tech High gets it right. What I think is most impressive about the school is not the technology—in fact, I think it's misnamed; it should be called Great Teaching High—but the teachers who use the technology. Of course, the school couldn't do a lot of the things it does without the technology, but it's the incredible teachers who make this school so special.

Conclusion

Unless we, as a country, make a commitment to rethinking our entire approach to human capital, we are never going to be able to take full advantage of the technological opportunities we have before us. The bottom line is that while I love technology—I couldn't teach effectively without it—our focus needs to be on people.

Reference

Walsh, K., D. Glaser, and D. Dunne Wilcox. 2006. *What education schools aren't teaching about reading and what elementary teachers aren't learning.* Washington, DC: National Council on Teacher Quality.

⬤ ⬤ ⬤ The Sound of Silence: Presidential Candidates and Technology for Tomorrow's Schools

Penelope M. Earley

The 2008 Presidential Election and the Candidates' Positions

The 2008 election of the president of the United States will be unique in the history of this country. An unusually large number of individuals from both parties are declared candidates; they are politically diverse, with beliefs ranging from sharply minimizing the federal role in domestic policy to increasing it significantly; and, from the perspective of fall 2007, it would appear that the Democratic nominee will be either a woman or an African American. Yet perhaps the most important aspect of this election season is how early it began, with candidates announcing their decision to run over a year before the November 2008 election date. There are significant political consequences of these early announcements. Although candidates and their advisors may feel that additional exposure to the electorate will help them build momentum during the nomination process, lengthening campaigns has potential risks. With so many candidates in the field, the early state primaries and caucuses take on greater importance. Whoever wins in Iowa and New Hampshire will be the presumed nominee for each party, marginalizing states with later primaries or caucuses. Clearly early announcements provide substantial time for the candidates to attend and speak at public events and/or debates. For voters, this is an opportunity to get to know each of them better. For the candidates, however, the extended time frame presents more situations in which a political misstep could occur and be seized on by opponents and the media. Finally, it is possible that one or more of the candidates will peak too soon, and by the 2008 general election, the public will be tired of the campaign and make their weariness known by not voting.

Dr. Penelope M. Earley is Director of the Center for Education Policy and Professor at the College of Education and Human Development at George Mason University in Fairfax, Virginia.

With a crowded field of presidential candidates, there is pressure on each to present their positions on the issues they believe are most important to potential voters, and all have statements of one kind or another on education, although some are more expansive than others. During September 2007, the Web sites, blogs, speeches, and interviews for declared Democratic and Republican candidates were analyzed to determine their plans—if any—related to technology and tomorrow's schools. This analysis revealed that no candidate discussed schools of the future, nor did any reference the role or use of technology to improve student learning or achievement. Most candidates were on record commenting on pre-K–16 education, and the comments are characterized as follows:

- Fully fund the No Child Left Behind Act
- Modify the No Child Left Behind Act
- Eliminate the No Child Left Behind Act
- Support salary increases for teachers
- Support teacher professional development
- Support access to higher education
- Support pre-K education
- Maintain a strong economy by having good schools

Looking at candidates' statements on technology revealed no specific connection with education nor schools of the future, although at least one noted that technology is important for the health of the economy. While it can be argued that the connection between education and the economy and the ties between technology and the economy create a framework to think about new uses of technology in the schools, it is a very tenuous one.

For educators who believe that it is time for thoughtful conversations about what will characterize schools of tomorrow and the promise of technology to create 24/7 learning communities, the lack of attention to the future by the candidates offers an opportunity. With that in mind, I offer the following open letter to the next president of the United States.

An Open Letter to the Next President of the United States

Dear President Number 44:

During the campaign you were silent on the role of technology in tomorrow's schools. Now that you are about to assume the presidency of the United States, I write to urge you to use the power of your office to begin substantive discussions on how the schools of the future will differ from the schools of today. I offer the following points to begin this discussion.

Resist the notion that new technologies will fix an out-of-date school system. In 1957 the Soviet Union launched Sputnik, and the United States government responded by legislating the National Defense Education Act, which dedicated substantial federal funds for mathematics, science, and foreign language programs. Yet the elementary and secondary schools of 2007 are not fundamentally different from the schools of 1957. Students typically attend classes for 180 days a year. Generally they arrive between 7:00 a.m. and 8:00 a.m. and leave around 2:30 or 3:00 in the afternoon. They sit at desks in rooms, and one or more adults offer instruction. In some schools, chalkboards have been replaced by SMART Boards, and desks and chairs are no longer bolted to the floor, but little else has changed. While schools are efficient places to put children for seven hours while parents work or do other things, they are less efficient at preparing children to engage in complex problem solving and reasoning. Inserting new technologies into an out-of-date system will not yield the success we expect.

Resist the idea that new technologies will fix previous policy miscues. Children, schools, communities, and states are not homogeneous, and a new generation of computers or other technologies will not make them so. Arguably, technology must be deliberately linked with school reform, but it cannot mend the stress points caused by legislation such as the No Child Left Behind Act. It is important to consider policy options that truly allow us to think globally and act locally. Technology can help us do this through the creation of electronic learning communities that ignore city, state, or national boundaries.

There are many ways in which government can support innovative schools of tomorrow. The federal government has the unique power to protect the civil rights of its citizens and to invest substantial funds in areas of national priority. It is this ability to invest and stimulate the creation of new knowledge that will best serve the schools of tomorrow. As an example, the federal government should invest in the development of programs that use technology to create learning communities and to nurture inquiry and innovation. This should include supporting interdisciplinary research in neuroscience, technology, and pre-K–16+ education. It must be acknowledged that this research will not be expected to find the definitive "magic bullet" for restructuring education. Rather, this basic research should be structured to continually generate and test new learning theories. Innovative research is not done only through experimental design, in which students or schools are randomly assigned to either receive a particular form of instruction or not and then statistically compared. Innovation and invention should generate new knowledge: the Wright brothers did not have a control group.

Resist the notion that technology is best used only to prepare scientists, engineers, and mathematicians. Technology can be used to help students develop self-regulation skills to work in any field, either alone or as part of a nonproximate learning community. Technology can help students develop complex problem-solving and reasoning skills in subjects ranging from art to algebra.

Schools of the future will use technology to help students develop the flexibility to adapt to change and learn how to consider and use new information. This will be essential for evaluating the quality of information found on the Internet and engaging in important conversations on the scope of First Amendment privileges. Moreover, as communities begin to allow online voting, technology in educational settings can help students learn how to weigh information about candidates and vote as informed citizens.

An array of assistive technologies is now available to help children with disabilities learn. It is appropriate for the federal government to support further research in this area. It also is appropriate for the federal government to assist schools that lack resources to purchase equipment for their students. As scientific and medical advances occur, we will be able to identify children with a greater variety of learning styles and needs. Technology-rich schools of the future—such as The Online Academy—will be able to provide customized instruction for all children.

In 2007 Congress passed and the president signed the America COMPETES Act, which authorizes federal funds to support graduate students in mathematics and science, just as the National Defense Education Act did in 1958. If it is a national priority to increase the number of mathematicians and scientists, it may be a better use of federal resources to support a system of universal preschool for children, designed to instill in them a sense of curiosity that will lead them to successful careers in scientific fields as well as to careers as teachers, artists, nurses, public servants, or poets.

Resist the notion that we need to recruit more instructors. Recently there has been extensive debate over what it is that teachers need to know and be able to do. Scholars and advocates generally align themselves with one of two camps: those who believe it is important for teachers to have deep knowledge of the subject to be taught and those who emphasize preparation in how to teach the subject. Neither will be sufficient in the schools of tomorrow.

The next generation of teachers must be prepared to teach children who are "digital natives." These educators will need to have the proper skills to be facilitators of learning, not merely individuals who spoon-feed information to their students. They will need skills to help children learn to be explorers and inventors. Placing even the most sophisticated technology in a classroom will not make a less effective teacher better. As the schools of tomorrow evolve, current teachers will need to think about teaching and learning in new ways. This may lead to innovative ways of staffing schools that pair educators with different skills to work in teams. Another role for technology will be establishing interactive learning communities for teachers to share their own research on best practices and classroom strategies.

Realize the important link between technology and education reform. Technology plays a central role in new 24/7 lifelong learning and teaching systems. The Online Academy is an example of a way to deliver high school instruction that is customized for each student and available 24/7. Real-world learning, flexible scheduling, and mentor support characterize The Online Academy and illustrate how school reform and technology are linked.

The Online Academy (TOA)
A Virtual High School

Real-World Learning

TOA is based on a learning system that situates learning within the real world. Problems provide a shared learning activity that structures the learner's interactions with the instructional resources and provides a common focus for the interactions of the learner and the expert mentor. Problems serve as the guiding organizer of learning and instruction. The learner begins by studying the problem, seeking to understand the advice given about how to proceed. Depending on the needs of the expert mentor and the learner, all types of interactions may be structured by (but not limited to) one or more of the following: e-mail, telephone, face-to-face meetings, videoconferencing, and synchronous communications (instant messaging, chat room).

Scheduling

Students may register and complete a course or module at any time and according to their own pace. Each course is designed to be a full credit. Students may complete as much of the course as they need. The only timeline or deadline that must be followed is the timetable for taking the Virginia Standards of Learning test for the course or stipulations as defined by the cooperating school district.

Mentor Support

Expert mentors are assigned to learners as models and coaches for appropriate instructional periods from a single representative problem through a set sequence of problems. Expert mentors are not responsible for managing or monitoring the learner. Rather, expert mentors serve as models and coaches, offering assistance upon request; providing feedback on products submitted by the learner(s); asking prompting, extending, and application questions; and performing other assorted interactions to support learning. Every mentor in The Online Academy is a highly qualified teacher holding valid state licensure. http://toa.gmu.edu

---

In conclusion, the schools of tomorrow may not be schools at all, but learning communities linked across distances by technology. These learning communities should serve not only as rich environments for interactive learning and discovery, but as a mechanism to help equalize access to instructional resources.

Respectfully yours,
Penelope Earley
Citizen, Parent, Grandparent, and Educator

⬤ ⬤ ⬤   Learning 3.0: Where Do We Go from Here?

Tom Welch

Like most districts in the country, the Quabbin Regional School District is facing a critical issue. With all of the possibilities that technology holds, coupled with the tremendous frustrations that young people are experiencing, many of us are left with this idea of "Now what?" We may understand that there are difficulties with implementation, and that there are solutions that perhaps lie beyond our reach, but what can we do now? The title of this paper is a play on Thomas Friedman's concept of Globalization 3.0 (2005). Learning 3.0 represents the transition from an industrial-based model of education to a knowledge-based model—an idea most districts are not even really thinking about, as they're still trying to tweak everything they can out of the industrial-based model. Education reformer Horace Mann was born just 75 miles from the Quabbin Reservoir, propelling Massachusetts—the backbone of the industrial age—toward being the state that introduced the school age to the rest of the country.

It's 2007, and there is no reason why geography continues to be the most important factor in determining what any child in this country can achieve and has access to in terms of educational equity. It's 2007, and every student should have the opportunity to learn in a place like High Tech High. The most important question educators need to ask themselves is: Are we going to be in the school business, or are we going to be in the learning business? In 2007, those are two very different things.

The Business of School

Twenty or even forty years ago, how long did it take a student to move through fourth grade? One year. And today, how long does it take a student to get through that grade? One year. With all of the hundreds of thousands of dollars that we've invested over the years in technology and professional development—all that we know about brain research, all that we know about learning styles, all that we have invested in to become better at this craft—it still takes a student the same amount of time as it did before.

Tom Welch is President of T. Welch Consulting in Lexington, Kentucky, and senior consultant for CCSSO and the International Center for Leadership in Education.

This scenario makes some sense if you're in the school business because school is set up in years. But if you really want to use technology to transform your district into a learning system, you're going to need to think about the idea of school in a completely different way. You've got the infrastructure there, and with that infrastructure you can go in two separate directions: you can continue to be in the school business and use it to reinforce everything that you've been doing, or you can use it to transition into the learning business.

If we think about the changes in industry over the last few years, the words *faster*, *better*, and *cheaper* come to mind. We usually tell businesspeople that they can count on two of the three. They can get it fast and cheap, but it won't be high quality. Or they can get a high-quality item faster, but it won't be cheap. Imagine if someone had come to your automobile manufacturing business thirty years ago and said, "We're going to introduce millions of dollars worth of technology into your business with these guarantees: You'll still be able to turn out the same number of cars every year, but you will have the advantage of being able to invest in a lot of professional development and training for the people using that technology. Plus, the cars that you'll be turning out will still have the same number of defects and rejects that you had before." It's hard to imagine anyone thinking that this was a great deal, and yet this is exactly what we have allowed to happen in education. School districts need to ask themselves, "Can we use technology not just to reinforce what we've been doing but to create a learning system instead of a school system?" And if that's going to be done, they're going to need to design things differently.

With the rare exception, school years are about 180 days long. Where did that number come from? There's nothing magic about 180 days being the amount of time kids need to be able to learn a certain amount of content. There is, however, something about 180 days being the magic number both for paying people to come in and teach, and for giving kids a period of time for learning and a period of time for play. There are no doubt policies in every district or state that say the school day will be anywhere from 6 to 7.5 hours long. Part of this is in response to the Committee of Ten's Carnegie Unit—a concept originally developed to determine which college professors would qualify for full retirement benefits but which established the course of secondary education in the process.

This is a holdover from the industrial age, where we thought in terms of place—the factory. We put workers in a factory and made them use a time card—the most important tool for measuring performance in a factory. Workers would start work at seven in the morning and quit at five in the evening. They didn't get paid for any time before seven or after five, and as long as their supervisor thought they were doing an adequate job, they got paid for all their time in between. So the reward for these workers was the wage, and it was based on time. Put in a school context, the place becomes the school building. In the industrial age, it made perfect sense to send students to school because that's where the knowledge was—that's where the books were, that's where the people who knew more things than the people at home were. Time, just like in the factory, was ordered around the bell. You weren't to be evaluated on anything before the bell rang, or on anything after. Unless it was happening during that class time, students were not going to get credit for it. And that credit—transferring to the next grade—was the payback. And the quality didn't matter so much as long as your immediate supervisor—your teacher—thought that you were doing okay. This is why we've ended up in the situation we're in now.

Transitioning to a Learning Business

Today we can look at the change to the knowledge-based economy where we take the work to the workers and ask ourselves how we can apply this to a knowledge-based learning system. With all of the infrastructure there, do kids really have to go to school to learn? Take foreign languages, for example. Today there are some really amazing Web sites available for teaching languages online. Languagelab.com offers an immersion course using culturally authentic materials. Assessments are given, and learners can speak with people from the country of origin. In most schools, if a student can't get into the 9:32 a.m. German class, he or she is out of luck. With the access that we have to technology, it doesn't have to be that way.

Current Policies

Many people think that technology and the implementation of technology for learning happens at the classroom level. From a policy position, I would contend that the most important things happen at the district and state levels. When I talk about policy regarding the use of technology, most people think, "Yes, we've got policies in place; we have our AUP—our Acceptable Use Policy." Several areas of policy currently exist. First are the restrictive policies, which would cover things like the AUP. These policies are absolutely necessary for keeping our students safe and making sure that they're using technology responsibly.

The second type of policy is also restrictive but is based in fear. There are districts across the country in which students can't do many of the things available to them because the Internet sites are blocked. These kinds of restrictive policies serve to cut us off from some amazing learning opportunities. Today we have many aspects of our presidential campaign being decided by YouTube, and yet there are history classes all over the country in which students—and even teachers—can't access YouTube.

I remember the first time I was faced with something like this. It was the day after the 2000 presidential elections, when the winner of the race was still undecided. I was a high school principal at the time, and I thought, "This must be a great day for my AP U.S. history teacher." Imagine my surprise when I walked into his classroom and found him talking about Reconstruction. And I said, "Eddie! What are you doing? This is one of the most important days in U.S. history!" He answered, "Well, this is what was in my lesson plans, and so this is what I'm supposed to be teaching today."

I'm not saying that there ought to be open season on every site that there is on the Internet, but the policies have to look at how we're determining what's possible and what's not. And we need to keep up with what's available. In this time of ever-quickening technological developments, creating an ethics course for our kids is extremely important. Five years ago it was cell phones; today it's YouTube and Facebook. What is it going to be tomorrow? Are we going to remain one step behind our kids in terms of what they are accessing, or are we going to give them the tools to begin to become responsible users of the technology that's there? Besides which, we may be able to keep them off some of those sites while they're in school, but unless we've given them the background to know about how to make wise, safe decisions as individuals, they'll be at the mercy of the wolves when they're away from school, because most of them have access to technology in much different ways. A really important thing to consider for a district is an ethics course in twenty-first-century technology.

The third type of policy is learner based. These policies define the standards for each class as well as the assessments that will be used to determine whether learning has actually occurred.

When I first started my principalship, every teacher in the school gave his or her own version of a final exam. Then we moved to the point where every teacher teaching the same subject gave the same final exam. Finally we moved to the point where no student could pass a course without passing the final exam for that course. Some people were outraged by this because they said that some students were in classes without the requisite skills to be there. This was discovered first in a mathematics course, in which there were many students who didn't have the background to succeed. Part of the reason for this was that some teachers were using extra credit in their math classes that had nothing to do with actual learning in the class—for example, if you brought in enough canned goods for the FFA Thanksgiving Food Drive, you could pass the course. And so the teachers finally came to the conclusion that it was immoral for them to set up a kid to fail when they knew the kid wasn't going to have the tools needed to go on to the next level. And the first year they did that, only four kids failed—four out of a one thousand-student high school. As you move from a school system to a learning system, you must define what it is kids are going to be learning, and you must create assessments that will determine the quality of that product.

Creating a Learning Business through Policy

Tier-One Policies

When it comes to technology, you have to take the limits off of your school day and your school year. Learning can occur 24/7/7—twenty-four hours a day, seven days a week, across seven continents. Children can learn anytime, anywhere, and that's what you should be encouraging them to do.

The second policy is the use of an online individualized learning plan. An outstanding example is happening in Kentucky, starting in fifth grade and continuing past high school. This plan is a tremendous tool, starting out with a student interest inventory and continuing through each year. It's fully integrated with the postsecondary system, which is absolutely vital for student success.

The third policy, which a lot of people won't be ready for, is a move toward performance-based credentialing. This acknowledges the absurdity of the idea that it magically takes a year to learn X amount of content. We all know that that is a random notion, but we haven't had a system in place to accommodate it. Part of the reason was that we didn't have the standards, we didn't have the assessments, to know whether learning had actually occurred. In Kentucky right now, high school students are taking virtual language classes. Students get their two credits when they perform at a certain proficiency level on a recognized performance-based computer-adaptive assessment—and it doesn't matter if it takes them six months or three years. Should it take every fourth grader exactly one year to move through the grade? Not when many of them have access to the type of technology you could make available to them through your servers.

In Kentucky, there are currently one hundred fourth and fifth graders in Algebra 1. At the end of the course, they'll be taking the same Algebra 1 assessment that kids all over the state take, and they'll be credited when they pass. Kids deserve to be moving faster. There are kids in every single district in this country who either can move faster and deserve that opportunity or need more time and deserve that chance. And the way to give them more time is not to say at the end of the year, "Stop. Put down your pencils. You get an 'F.' Go back to 'Go.'" The way to do it is to say, "Okay—we're performance based. We're extending your year until you learn this material." That's what we're about in Kentucky. We're no longer a school system but a learning system.

The fourth policy involves appropriate advancement. If it doesn't take a fourth grader a whole year to move through fourth grade, what do we do with that student in April when he or she is ready to move on? At my high school, we had teachers in four core areas loop with the students for two years, so if a kid finished Algebra 1 in April, he or she stayed with that teacher, and I didn't have to find another class for them to move to. Technology was a real key because students understood that they could be responsible for the rate at which they were learning, and that we would open up other opportunities for them if they learned more rapidly. What started out as an experiment proved to be tremendously successful for those kids.

The fifth policy involves portfolio responsibility. Electronic portfolios should be kept so that you can track your students' learning and authenticate that the learning has occurred. This is a very important consideration—not just a scrapbook—and it should be part of the individual learning plan that's already online.

Tier-Two Policies

These policies are a little trickier, involving things such as determining what class rank means in the context of technology. If you have one student who has taken every class offered at your high school and has earned 32 credits in a four by four block, with all As, how are you going to determine his or her class rank when compared to the student who has earned 50 credits because he or she earned 18 of them online—at night or during the summer? These are the questions that'll eat up the school board's time with parents of the student who did everything by the book versus parents of the student who was learning on his or her own.

And then come the tertiary connections after secondary school—you want to make sure that you have appropriate relationships developed with your postsecondary institutions in the area. Part of Kentucky's new graduation requirement is that every student not only has to complete Algebra 2 but has to take math every year. It used to be that you could take geometry and Algebra 2 and you were done, and if you started in eighth grade, you were done with math by tenth grade; therefore, many kids didn't have math the last two years of high school. So now what in the learning system is a teacher going to do when he has fifth graders who have finished Algebra 1? What are you going to do in your middle school with sixth graders who need geometry? Most middle schools are not teaching geometry. What are you going to do about teacher certification when you have kids ready for German 3 who are in seventh grade and you don't even offer German 3 in your district? These are the sort of problems I'd love to have on a regular basis. How do we keep up with student learning in a twenty-first-century environment?

Conclusion

One of the projects that I'm currently working on with the Council of Chief State School Officers is the establishment of a system of national virtual-learning magnet schools, so that any child in the country will be able to have a magnet school education no matter where he or she lives. The first one will be the National Virtual Learning Magnet for Space, Science and Mathematics in cooperation with NASA, which will provide every student with a laptop.

It is a new day. Those working in the Quabbin Regional School District are lucky to be in a district that is looking forward—that's thinking about setting themselves up as a learning district rather than a school district.

Reference

Friedman, T. L. 2005. *The world is flat: A brief history of the twenty-first century.* New York: Farrar, Straus and Giroux.

⚫ ⚫ ⚫ Working Toward Flexibility in the Age of Technology

Sue M. Gee

According to Peter Senge,

> A simple question to ask is, "How has the world of a child changed in the last 150 years?" And the answer is, "It's hard to imagine any way in which it hasn't changed." Children know more about what's going on in the world today than their teachers, often because of the media environment they grow up in. They're immersed in a media environment of all kinds of stuff that was unheard of 150 years ago, and yet if you look at school today versus 100 years ago, they are more similar than dissimilar. (Newcomb 2003)

Therefore, the key to preparing teachers for this new world of schooling with new kinds of students is flexibility. Employers are looking for employees who can adapt to changing needs, juggle multiple responsibilities, multitask, and routinely make decisions on their own. Technology in advanced communications has transformed the world into a global community. The world, in essence, is flat.

The technology architecture of the future must be flexible, too. The basic foundation, the network that holds up all of the innovative devices, some of which are yet to be invented, must be one that can adapt to the changing tools that will emerge. Not only will teachers need basic technology skills, but they will also need to be more adaptable and more flexible. The emphasis for teachers will be on teaching students how to learn, how to think, and how to solve problems. This will require a shift to students with more independent learning capabilities—self-directed students who know where they need to go to get the answers they need to accomplish the task at hand.

The Quabbin Regional School District is taking all of this into consideration as we embark on a plan for enhancing the technology infrastructure in a 3,200-student, six-building district spread over a large geographical area in rural Massachusetts. We don't yet know exactly what we need, and in fact, we may not ever know this as completely as we might have in the past.

Sue Gee is the Superintendent of the Quabbin Regional School District, which is made up of five towns: Barre, Hubbardston, Hardwick, New Braintree, and Oakham. Her office is in Barre, Massachusetts.

How, then, do we even talk about the changes that we cannot yet envision in a way that will engender trust in our stakeholders? How will we move teachers to a more flexible teaching approach, away from the concrete-sequential world that is familiar to schooling? Are the teachers who arrive tomorrow from colleges and universities ready for this new media environment? These are just a few of the questions that we are grappling with as we begin this project.

Reference

Newcomb, Amelia. 2003. Peter Senge on organizational learning. *School Administrator*, May.

⬤ ⬤ ⬤ Restructuring Our Schools to Keep Up with Our Students

Richard Paula

Introduction

The Quabbin Regional School District is grappling with a number of issues. We started a school renovation project about eighteen years ago and, as of ten years ago, have remodeled or rebuilt all of our schools, incorporating most of the technology redevelopment into our middle and high schools. When I started at my elementary school, we were using Apple IIs with floppy drives, and the idea of a network and the Internet was nonexistent.

We recently put together a presentation to give our school committee members an idea of what our students faced. We wanted to make the point that kids at home have far more technology available to them than we have in our classrooms, and that we need to focus on more fully equipping our classrooms.

History

Throughout the past decade, we've embarked on some small technology initiatives. Generally there's now a computer in every classroom, although we're still using computer labs, typically manned by media specialists on fixed schedules. We have wired classrooms and wireless access, as well as mobile carts—each of which holds twelve computers. In our elementary school, we have one mobile cart for approximately 120 students—primarily fifth and sixth graders. In our middle school, there's one cart for 600 students, and at our high school, one cart for 700 students.

Basically what we're seeing are teachers using technology to support traditional instruction, doing much of the same thing that the previous generation of teachers have done: stand in front of the room and lecture, while using technology as a side benefit. Alternatively, they're sending their students down to the library to "go find facts," because before there was Google, there were librarians.

Richard Paula is Media Specialist at Ruggles Lane School in Barre, Massachusetts.

Some librarians want to remain the keepers of the hallowed books, while some want to transform the library into a version of Starbucks, in which students can wander around and gather their own information, with the librarian standing by to help. These kinds of discussions are happening everywhere.

Our students are predominately being lectured to. They don't have the real-world experiences that we know they need, and there are few opportunities for students to build their own instruction. We do have some people who are starting to experiment with wikis and blogs, but they are few and far between.

Goals for the Future

What we want to do is move toward integrating information and letting students learn wherever and whenever they can, and find that particular piece of information for themselves. We need to engage them and challenge them at their level, while responding to their needs. Differentiated instruction is important, but we also want to work with timely feedback, to make sure parents as well as students know where they're going and how they can improve. Our student instruction needs to consist of engaging in-depth lessons rather than just focusing on specific skills at a cursory level. We want to drill down and make sure students get a real understanding of a topic so that they can then use those skills to produce a product that they can then use to both demonstrate their depth of knowledge and teach others. We're also looking for students to engage in real-life experiences rather than just doing activities out of a book.

Today's students learn differently; they're more plugged in visually. Whenever my students are given the choice between working on a project or doing a worksheet, the project always wins hands down. These students crave direct practical experience—they want to build and do rather than listen and read—and we need to be able to provide them with the tools to get it.

⬤ ⬤ ⬤ The Importance of State Virtual Schools to State Academic Goals

William Thomas

The nonprofit Southern Regional Education Board (SREB) was created in 1948 by southern governors and legislatures to improve the quality of education in the south. We work with sixteen member states from Delaware to Texas, and are located on the campus of Georgia Tech. Everything we do is from a K–20 perspective, looking at academics first, then state policy, then technology. About fourteen years ago, the SREB formed the Educational Technology Cooperative—a group of representatives from each of the sixteen states' departments of education as well as agencies responsible for governing or conducting higher education, including boards of regents, coordinating boards, and higher education commissions. The representatives from those thirty-seven agencies work together on a wide range of educational technology issues.

One of the areas that we have focused a lot of attention on over the last several years has been online learning. We're working with states because education is a state responsibility. We work very closely with our governors and our legislators on a wide range of issues, including those involving technology. We have to remember where we are within our sixteen states; we represent 800 public two- and four-year institutions, as well as about 3,400 school districts. We have some very large districts, such as Dade County, Houston Unified, and Fairfax County, and also have districts where the schools are so small the superintendent drives the school bus. With these kinds of differences, it doesn't make sense to assume that everyone is going to be able to do the same things in their school systems. We need to pay attention to each district's particular needs.

State Virtual Schools

Florida Virtual School (FLVS) was created back in 1997 as a small grant-based program between two Florida districts. This past academic year, FLVS had 55,000 middle and high school students successfully

William R. Thomas is Director of Educational Technology for the Southern Regional Education Board in Atlanta, Georgia.

complete online courses. I use the word "successfully" because FLVS is treated like a school district, as a result of state legislation handed down about four years ago. That legislation stated that Florida Virtual School will get a portion of the total full-time equivalency for every student who successfully completes a course as defined by the state of Florida. Therefore, the school is 100 percent performance based. When Kentucky Virtual School was created back in 2000, the state board of education waived seat-time requirements for any student taking a course at Kentucky Virtual School. In fact, not one of the virtual schools in our sixteen-state region has seat-time requirements.

The West Virginia Virtual School was created in 2000. At about the same time, the West Virginia legislature passed a bill saying that every middle school student in West Virginia would have access to a foreign language. Though this seemed like a good idea on paper, the trouble was that West Virginia has a lot of tiny middle schools out in the middle of nowhere. To think that they were all going to offer even one foreign language, much less multiple ones, seemed absurd. As a result, West Virginia Virtual School partnered with Florida Virtual School and created Spanish I and II, which they began offering to middle school students—and they have been very successful. Several years ago the U.S. Department of Education chose to evaluate this West Virginia implementation as part of a larger three-year scientific study. Results of that portion of the study showed that middle school students in West Virginia taking online foreign language did as well as or better than their face-to-face counterparts (West Virginia Department of Education 2006). In fact, most of the virtual schools in our region have between an 80 and a 90 percent completion rate. And the majority of the remaining 10 to 20 percent are made up of students who drop a course because they find it too difficult—much more difficult than a similar course taken in their face-to-face schools.

Governor Mark Warner wanted to create a virtual school in Virginia because he wanted to be sure that students across the commonwealth had access to AP courses. Statistics from the College Board indicate that about 40 percent of high schools across the country do not offer AP courses. A couple of the states in our region passed state codes over the last few years saying that every high school will need to offer one or two AP courses by a certain date. According to that College Board report, the virtual schools in our region offer thirty-one separate AP courses. The College Board offers testing on a total of thirty-seven AP courses. Theoretically, with the virtual school, any high school anywhere could offer thirty-seven different AP courses, whether that school has five hundred or fifty students. If there's one student in a school who needs it, he or she could have access to whatever foreign language he or she wanted, including Mandarin Chinese, which at least four of our virtual schools now offer.

As for the other SREB states, Delaware's legislature just passed legislation, and the state is working on a plan right now. Texas passed initial legislation, and Tennessee invested over $2 million—mostly in federal funds—to develop online courses, with the intent of implementing them next year.

In Florida, there is a citizen watchdog organization called Florida Tax Watch, which has been around for about thirty years. This group watches the legislature and the governor on an ongoing basis, and any time a bill gets passed and signed by the governor that it believes the citizens of Florida should be concerned about, the group gives it a "turkey."

Back in the late nineties, Florida Virtual School almost got a turkey because it was new and very few people knew about it. About a year ago, some members of the legislature and others went to the watchdog group requesting its third-party perspective on Florida Virtual. The group took this on and spent a year reviewing Florida Virtual School from all perspectives, including academics, student populations, minorities served (30%), and cost. As a result of its review, the group produced a 91-page document saying that Florida Virtual is an outstanding opportunity for students across the state in terms of academics, as well as a good buy for Florida's students (2007).

Policy Changes

Policy is ultimately going to be the driving force behind a lot of what we're talking about. We have found that to be absolutely true as regards the SREB states, whether it's putting the right policies in place or removing old brick-and-mortar policies that have no business in the twenty-first century. Seat-time requirements are certainly a great example of that, but there are many others. The SREB works very closely with its legislators and governors, and has talked with them about online learning over the last seven or eight years now. At a legislative meeting in 1999 or 2000, we were in the midst of a presentation about online learning, both K–12 and higher education, and one legislator from Virginia—a lawyer who also taught online law courses from one of the campuses in the Tidewater area—commented, "You know, I know my online students so much better than I know my face-to-face students." Later in the session, another legislator from Virginia interrupted us and said, "I still don't quite understand what you're telling us. Are you trying to say that a student can sit in front of a computer and take a course for academic credit?" So those are the extremes that we're dealing with. And though we are still dealing with a lack of understanding on a certain level, the need for a major cultural change is upon us. We have often been asked why so many SREB states have state virtual schools or are moving in that direction. It's clear to us that these states have been sharing information.

An important point to make to those who feel scared or threatened by this movement is that none of the state virtual schools offer a diploma. They're not high schools, and they're not trying to replace high schools. What they're doing is filling in the gaps. At every school—and I don't care if it's the wealthiest school in the state—there are students who need courses that are not being offered. A virtual school program allows for that opportunity to occur. And for many, it's far beyond that. Virginia Virtual offers twenty different AP courses, and the person in charge of it, Cathy Cheeley, said to me that probably 75 percent of the kids who took AP courses last year would never have had the opportunity to take even one had it not been for Virginia Virtual. This is one of the reasons people are promoting the use of state virtual schools.

The professional standards commission did a study several years ago in which it identified somewhere in the neighborhood of 80 to 82 certified physics teachers in the entire state of Georgia—a state containing over four hundred high schools. So it's clear that without Georgia Virtual, a lot of kids in Georgia would not have access to either physics at all or physics with a teacher who was fully certified. The online program offers that to any student at any time.

Funding is clearly a big issue. In fact, we're convening a meeting at the SREB next month to look at funding alternatives for state virtual schools, because many of them—West Virginia, Kentucky, Georgia—currently have a cap, which prevents them from meeting the needs of many students.

Gene Wilhoit—executive director of the Council of Chief State School Officers (CCSSO)—was an SREB board member until late 2006, about the time he left his post as Kentucky's commissioner of education. At one of our meetings he made a comment about how when he first learned about online learning in virtual schools, he thought it was a good thing—a little something on the side—but that he now realizes that for education reform and for all the things we need to do for our kids in the twenty-first century, online learning has to be front and center. Wilhoit has seen the changes taking place and recognizes the importance of online learning for the state of Kentucky.

Credit recovery is an important issue to our states. In addition, many states are increasing high school graduation requirements, including Delaware, where they are requiring two years of foreign language. Many policy makers know that some of the school districts are not going to be able to meet that requirement without the Delaware Virtual School, so they're connecting the dots. This isn't about technology. Technology is the way to get what we're talking about, but this is all about the right policies, addressing the right cultural issues. The biggest barrier to online education is people—people who either don't understand it or consider it too much work to implement. If we are serious about student learning, we need to work on changing the culture.

References

Florida Tax Watch. 2007. Final report: A comprehensive assessment of Florida Virtual School. www.floridataxwatch.org/resources/pdf/110507FinalReportFLVS.pdf.

Southern Regional Education Board. 2007. State virtual schools—successes and growing pains. http://www.sreb.org/programs/EdTech/pubs/pubsindex.asp.

West Virginia Department of Education. 2006. Research findings from the West Virginia Virtual School Spanish Program. http://wvde.state.wv.us/techworkplan/Ed%20Pace%20Research%20Brief.pdf.

⬤ ⬤ ⬤   Use of Technology and Music to Improve Learning

Ronald A. Berk

DISCLAIMER: *This chapter can in no way replicate the original presentation with slide custom animation, transitions, and forty-five music clips in a PowerPoint production. Instead, the content will be covered and expanded tenfold, with a research review and the music recommendations cited, where appropriate. Your reading will be more informative but considerably less entertaining than if you were experiencing the presentation. Enjoy!*

This chapter examines what we know and don't know about music and learning. Specific outcomes and techniques to integrate music into teaching are proffered. Like ancient Gaul, the chapter is divided into five sections:*

1. Why use music in teaching?
2. Technology tools in the classroom
3. Selecting appropriate music
4. Ten generic techniques for using music in teaching
5. Finale

See you at the finale.

Why Use Music in Teaching?

When you watch a TV program or movie, your feelings and emotions—such as excitement, anger, laughter, relaxation, love, whimsy, or even boredom—are often triggered or heightened by the music playing behind the action. You are responding to the mood created by the music and the scene. The soundtrack is so powerful that you may download it off the Internet or order the CD from Amazon so that you can listen to it

---

*Sidebar: Gaul was divided into three parts, you knucklehead! *Oops.*

Dr. Ronald A. Berk is Professor Emeritus of Biostatistics and Measurement at Johns Hopkins University. He can be reached at www.ronberk.com or rberk@sonjhmi.edu.

again and relive the experience. This attraction to soundtracks extends to Broadway musicals and classical, jazz, rhythm and blues, rock, pop, and new-age music concerts as well. So how can teachers use music as an instructional tool in ways that students will want a CD soundtrack of their classes?

Instructional Outcomes

The entertainment value of music has been demonstrated. The key question here is: Why isn't there a soundtrack to accompany this chapter? That's actually still in production, but that's not the question I was referring to. Instead, What is the learning value of music in the classroom? Here are twenty potential outcomes to ponder:

1. Grab students' attention
2. Focus students' concentration
3. Generate interest in class
4. Create a sense of anticipation
5. Establish a positive atmosphere/environment
6. Energize or relax students for learning exercise
7. Draw on students' imagination
8. Build rapport among students
9. Improve attitudes toward content and learning
10. Build a connection with other students and teacher
11. Increase memory of content/concepts
12. Facilitate the completion of monotonous, repetitive tasks
13. Increase understanding
14. Foster creativity
15. Improve performance on tests and other measures
16. Inspire and motivate students
17. Make learning fun
18. Augment celebration of successes
19. Set an appropriate mood or tone
20. Decrease anxiety and tension on scary topics

After you have finished pondering, consider the theoretical and research evidence related to these outcomes, which is reviewed and critiqued in the following two sections: (a) music and the brain, and (b) the effects of music on learning. This evidence furnishes the foundation not only for how music can be used as an effective teaching tool but, more important, for music's potential as a legitimate, systematic teaching method for all K–12 teachers.

Music and the Brain

There are a quadrillion volumes on the topic of the brain, especially the ones that begin with *This Is Your Brain on...* Specifically, the primary interest here is on how music is processed in students' brains to facilitate learning. This review covers: (1) core intelligences of musical/rhythmic and emotional, (2) left and right hemispheres, (3) triune brain, (4) brain-wave frequencies, and (5) music-brain conclusions.

Core intelligences. Among Gardner's (Gardner 1983, 1993, 1999, 2005; Gardner and Hatch 1989; Marks-Tarlow 1995; Williams, Blythe, White, Li, Sternberg, and Gardner 1996) 8.5 multiple intelligences, musical/rhythmic is one of the core intelligences in every student's brain. It involves appreciating and recognizing music, composing, keeping time, performing, recognizing rhythm, and singing. Despite the bevy of talentless contestants auditioning on *American Idol* year after year, which seems to seriously challenge Gardner's theory, he is pretty sure that everyone has that intelligence to some extent, it being part of the unique profile of strong and weak intelligences that every student possesses. Neuroscientific research has confirmed the physical difference in the neuronal networks of each student's brain (Zull 2002). Teachers can only work with what each student brings to the classroom.

This "pluralistic view of the mind" permits teachers to think of exposing their students to a wide range of learning strategies. Drawing on from four to six intelligences allows virtually every student to use their strong intelligences as well as to strengthen their weaker ones. Music should be one of those six.

Goleman's (1998) emotional intelligence is also tied to music. (Note: Gardner's intrapersonal and interpersonal intelligences are similar to Goleman's emotional intelligence.) Music elicits emotional reactions of liking or disliking and excitement or arousal (North and Hargreaves 1997; Robazza, Macaluso, and D'Urso 1994). It can be used to communicate with learners at a deeper level of understanding by touching their emotions.

Left and right hemispheres. There are separate hemispheres of the brain related to two ways of thinking: verbal and nonverbal (Gazzaniga 1992; Sperry 1973). The left hemisphere is predominately the logical and analytical side, which processes information sequentially, as in mathematics, logic, and language. It is also referred to as the verbal side, which is structured, factual, controlled, rational, organized, planned, and objective (Miller 1997). In contrast, the right hemisphere is the nonverbal, creative side, which is spontaneous, emotional, disorganized, experimental, empathetic, subjective, intuitive, and in search of relationships. It focuses on art, color, pictures, and music (Jourdain 1997; Polk and Kertesz 1993).

As you might have guessed, the educational system has emphasized the predominance of the left brain. Ergo, the plot of *Mr. Holland's Opus*, in which a high school music program gets cut in favor of more important, basic left brain courses and the athletic program. However, there seems to be an increasing appreciation for what the right brain can contribute to learning. The best news is that music taps both hemispheres. The left side processes rhythm and lyrics; the right side listens for melodies, sounds, and harmonic relationships over time (Bever and Chiarello 1974; Hébert and Peretz 1997; Schlaug et al. 1995). When children study music, the connections between the two hemispheres increase as they age (Schlaug et al. 1995). Clearly, music can be an effective tool for engaging both hemispheres.

Triune brain. A cross-section of the brain would reveal that it has three layers: (1) the stem, or *reptilian* brain (5%), which is responsible for such basic functions as breathing, blood pressure, and heartbeat, and determines the nature of sound—its direction, volume, and potential threat; (2) the inner layer, or *limbic* brain (10%), which is the center of our emotions and reacts to music with appropriate emotions and triggers long-term memory; and (3) the outer layer wrapper, or "bark," called the *neocortex* or *cerebral cortex* brain (85%)—which controls hearing, vision, language, and higher-level functioning, and responds to music intellectually (MacLean 1990). The latter "thinking brain" absorbs the sounds of the reptilian brain and the feelings of the limbic system and organizes them into music. This triune concept facilitates our understanding and creation of music.

Brain-wave frequencies. Another aspect of brain functioning is brain-wave frequencies. Among the four types of waves—delta, theta, alpha, and beta—that relate to various levels of consciousness, the alpha and beta have particular implications for music (and for fraternities on most college campuses). Delta waves represent deep sleep, when the waves are least like they are when we are fully awake. Theta waves represent shallow sleep, deep contemplation, and free-flowing creativity, which may be most characteristic of students when the teacher just talks. Alpha waves occur when students are in a relaxed state of awareness, such as after they wake up in class. The right hemisphere is primarily engaged in the alpha state when students are reading, studying, or reflecting. The emotions are dominant, and the left hemisphere's rationality drops out of sight temporarily. Slow, minor-key music fosters alpha waves. It relaxes the brain, which can be useful when reviewing content so that it passes into long-term memory (Millbower 2000).

Beta waves are the patterns of a fully awake mind, when the left hemisphere kicks into action. This is multitasking mode for the Net Generation, when they are functioning at optimum speed. Fast, up-tempo, major-key music can snap to attention students who are in a drifting alpha or meditative theta state, leaving them super alert and ready for whatever activities the teacher has planned (Millbower 2000).

Music-brain conclusions. The value of music as a teaching tool lies in its potential to do the following: (1) tap the core intelligences of musical/ rhythmic and emotional (interpersonal and intrapersonal); (2) engage both the left and right hemispheres; (3) appeal to the reptilian, limbic, and neocortex layers of the brain to sense the nature of sounds, react to music emotionally, and appreciate it intellectually; and (4) manipulate students' alpha and beta brain waves to relax or alert them for learning when they're not sleeping in delta- or theta-wave land. It would be a shame not to stir up these intelligences, hemispheres, layers, and waves in the classroom to promote learning. For an opposing perspective on the adequacy of the preceding cognitive neuroscientific findings and their implications for educational practice, see Waterhouse's (2006a, 2006b) critical review of the evidence.

The Effects of Music on Learning

Beyond what is known about how our brain functions, what research has been conducted specifically to determine whether music has any positive effect on learning, especially with regard to the outcomes listed at the beginning of the chapter? This section reviews the evidence on the following: (1) *Sesame Street*, (2) "Mozart Effect" or not, (3) "active" and "passive" concerts, and (4) music and learning by subject area.

Sesame Street. Have you watched the Emmy Award–winning *Sesame Street* recently? If you haven't, shame on you! It is the most effective educational children's program in history, give or take a month. For nearly forty years and more than 4,100 episodes broadcast in 120 countries, *Sesame Street* has used music almost nonstop throughout its programs in segments with live people, muppets, or animation; video clips of people and animals; and even in the extremely popular "Elmo's World." It is a key tool for teaching children basic academic and life skills. The lyrics are chock-full of content to help kids remember numbers, arithmetic, geometric forms, letters, words, cognitive processes, and classification. Catchy melodies and upbeat tempos excite children and keep their attention while slipping content into their long-term memory. Researchers found that when the music and action stopped—such as in scenes taking place on Sesame Street consisting of dialogue between adults—children stopped watching (Fisch and Truglio 2001).

This music-action formula to learning has not been kept secret by the production staff of *Sesame Street*. Yet how many K–12 teachers have taken advantage of these powerful learning effects? The time for waiting is up; the Net Generation demands it. Students today have minimal patience with content requirements and the attention span of goat cheese (Berk 2008). They want everything "now." These behaviors, however, are by choice. They can spend hours playing video games or participating in other activities in which they are interested (Prensky 2006); they just find most school subjects boring. Unless the content is on their radar screens, they can't stay with it.

These characteristics of the Net Geners suggest that teachers should consider the music-action formula *Sesame Street* uses for preschoolers. Teachers need to create elementary, middle, and high school student versions of *Sesame Street* in their live, face-to-face classrooms. The application of music will be a start to break the mold of traditional teaching practices.

"Mozart Effect" or not. There have been several studies on the effects of instrumental music on spatial-temporal reasoning. Couched within the context of neurophysiological theory (Leng and Shaw 1991), the first study by Rauscher, Shaw, and Ky (1993) found that listening to music and executing spatial tasks share neural pathways in the brain's cortex. The music serves to prime, or warm up, these neural transmitters for the subsequent execution of spatial reasoning tasks. This finding was referred to as the Mozart Effect, named after Beethoven's Fifth Symphony, which was used in the study. Wrong! It was a Mozart piano sonata. College students listening to the first movement of Mozart's Sonata for Two Pianos, K. 448, had a significant but short-lived (10–15 minutes) improvement in spatial reasoning. The researchers followed this up two years later with another study, which produced similar results (Rauscher, Shaw, and Ky 1995).

Rauscher, Shaw, Levine, Wright, Dennis, and Newcomb (1997) then investigated preschoolers who studied piano. They found that those children performed significantly better in spatial and temporal reasoning ability than those who spent the same amount of time learning to use computers. This work was extended by Graziano, Peterson, and Shaw (1999) with 237 second graders who had both piano keyboard training and innovative math software. Those children scored significantly higher on proportional math and fractions than the control group, which had no piano keyboard training. These results suggest that the spatial-temporal approach can be generalized to teach other math and science concepts.

Three other investigations by Rideout and Laubach (1996), Rideout and Taylor (1997), and Sarnthein, Stein, Rappelsberger, Petsche, Rauscher, and Shaw (1997) confirmed the Mozart Effect findings. The second study replicated the original 1993 study using two different spatial reasoning tasks. The other two were EEG coherence studies, which found that the presence of right frontal and left temporo-parietal activity induced by listening to Mozart carried over into two spatial-temporal tasks.

Others have attempted to replicate the effect with musical pieces from Yanni, whose music has similar properties to Mozart's; minimalist music by Philip Glass; music of the dance group Aqua; and pieces by Albinoni and Schubert. To date, however, there is no published research on the effect using any nonclassical musical selections. The most recent two-part study of the Mozart Effect used an up-tempo Mozart piece and a slow piece by Albinoni (Schellenberg et al. 2007). This research found that Canadian undergraduates performed better on the symbol search subtest after listening to up-tempo Mozart compared to slow Albinoni, and Japanese five-year-olds produced drawings that were more creative, energetic, and technically proficient after singing or hearing familiar children's songs than after hearing Mozart or Albinoni.

Despite many of the above results in support of the Mozart Effect, another series of studies by Stough, Kerkin, Bates, and Mangan (1994); Kenealy and Monseth (1994); Newman, Rosenbach, Burns, Latimer, Matocha, and Vogt (1995); and McKelvie and Low (2002) found no Mozart Effect. The first three studies concluded that a brief listening to classical music does not enhance the spatial problem-solving of college students; the last study found no effect for children with an average age of twelve. In fact, it has been difficult to reproduce the effect experimentally (Rauscher and Hinton 2006; Steele, Ball, and Runk 1997; Steele, Bass, and Crook 1999). No other researchers have been able to replicate the effect in a rigorous control-group study. Furthermore, other researchers have argued that the spatial intelligence increase is nothing more than a shift in the participants' arousal (Steele 2000; Thompson, Schellenberg, and Husain 2001) or their preference for the music (Nantais and Schellenberg 1999).

In order to make sense out of all of this confusion over whether a definitive Mozart Effect exists, Chabris (1999) conducted a meta-analysis of sixteen studies on the effect based on 714 subjects. He found a trivial increase of 1.4 general IQ points for all studies and a 2.1 increase for those that only used spatial intelligence, compared to the 1993 study (Rauscher et al.), which produced an increase of 8–9 points in spatial intelligence. Hetland (2000) then reviewed every Mozart study to date, with a combined total of 1,014 subjects. She concluded that Mozart listeners outperformed the comparison groups more often than would be expected by chance but with small effects, which could be attributed to gender, ethnicity, musical preference, training, and spatial ability. Most recently, Waterhouse (2006a, 2006b) argued that the use of music in instruction should not be based on the inadequate empirical support from the Mozart Effect studies.

Overall, the research reviews and the bulk of evidence from the foregoing studies attempting to search for a Mozart Effect to boost spatial intelligence indicate *trivial, nonsignificant, and nonreplicable findings* compared to the original study fifteen years ago (Rauscher et al. 1993). What's even more discouraging is the quality of research being conducted. Most of the investigations cited previously by Rauscher, Rideout, and Steele lack an independent control group, which precludes a comparison of scores between listening to Mozart and attempting spatial problems, measured only by the Stanford-Binet spatial subtest. Furthermore, many of the sample sizes were inadequate, and no demographic descriptors of the children or the college students participating in the research were provided, which could be correlates or explanations of IQ score increases.

"Active" and "passive" concerts. In the 1960s, Bulgarian psychiatrist Lozanov explored techniques to use music to increase learning and memory. The theories, research, and strategies he developed emerged into what is now known as accelerated learning (Lozanov 1978). The use of background music lies at the foundation of his techniques. Lozanov created two very different but equally effective learning environments, or concerts: active and passive.

An *active concert* activates the learning process mentally, physically, and/or emotionally by playing an up-tempo piece of music and reading or reciting language phrases in time with the music. This has been found to produce high memory retention. An active concert during movement activities can increase productivity, energize students, grab students' attention, and make learning fun.

A *passive concert* involves slower, Baroque-type music to relax the students' alpha brain-wave state and stabilize the students' mental, physical, and/or emotional rhythms to increase information absorption. Students enter into a relaxed state of awareness, opening their minds to incoming information. The music helps them maintain focus and concentration. By tapping into the pleasant emotions of the limbic system, information passes into long-term memory. Lozanov found that students could learn language skills at least four times faster via this approach compared with traditional methods; hence, the term "accelerated learning." Brewer

(1995) has recommended that background "passive" music can be played while students study, read, or write to increase attention levels, improve retention and memory, extend focused learning time, and expand thinking skills. This music can also be effective during reviews and tests.

Lozanov's techniques also included other ways to promote a positive learning environment, such as playing music as students enter and leave the classroom and during break times. (This is particularly appropriate for teachers who have a revolving door.) Playing music this way can set the tone or mood for the entire day (Sousou 1997; Stratton and Zalanowski 1994).

Music and learning by subject area. Since Lozanov's work, there has been a growing number of studies related to using music across the K–12 curriculum to increase learning. Based on Lozanov's research, several studies have examined the effects of background music on writing tasks (Hallam and Godwin 2000), behavior and mathematics performance (Hallum and Price 1998), reading (Brown 1986), memory and reading comprehension (Furnham and Bradley 1997; Mullikin and Henk 1985), and science (Davidson and Powell 1986).

Others have explored how music affects reading and mathematics performance (Gardiner et al. 1996), mathematics skills (Graziano, Peterson, and Shaw, 1999; Vaughn 2000), reading and verbal skills (Douglas and Willatts 1994; Ho, Cheung, and Chan 2003; Lamb and Gregory 1993), reading speed (Miller and Schyb 1989), spelling and phonological skills (Overy 2003), and creativity (Adaman and Blaney 1995; Mohanty and Hejmadi 1992). Butzlaff (2000) conducted a meta-analysis of twenty-four studies of music and reading and concluded that a strong association exists between music and performance on reading/verbal tests.

To date, there is a scarcity of research in all subjects, especially at the middle and high school levels. The evidence accumulated at the preschool and elementary school grades suggests that music used as a systematic teaching tool can have a positive effect on learning reading and mathematics. Further controlled, well-executed studies with adequate sample sizes are still necessary to confirm that suggestion and furnish a body of evidence at the secondary level to justify the pedagogical value of music in a variety of courses.

Technology Tools in the Classroom

Our culture has been flooded with burgeoning technology. It is almost impossible to keep up with all of the amazing products that keep hitting the streets. Among all of the tools currently available, which ones do students use, and which ones have potential for classroom use? The answers to those questions are examined in the following two sections: (1) tools of the trade for students, and (2) tools for the classroom. Of course, by the time this chapter has been published, the information in those sections will be out-of-date. In fact, it's probably a good idea to rip these pages out of the book and trash them. That's just the nature of the technology beast.

Tools of the Trade for Students

Today's Net Generation is so sophisticated in terms of technology that they have been branded *digital natives* (Prensky 2006). "Digital" is their native language. They are "native speakers" of the language of computers, video games, and the Internet. As you observe these students, you will notice wires coming out of every part of their body. Attached to those wires are MP3 players, iPods, iPhones or smart phones, PCs, and all the other tools of the digital age (Berk 2008).

That brings us to our first multiple-choice question:

1. What are they doing with all of this equipment?
    A. Listening to music.
    B. Playing PC/video games.
    C. Talking on iPhone.
    D. Sending e-mails or text messages (TMs).
    E. Watching videos and/or TV.
    F. Multitasking on at least 3 of the above.
    G. Multitasking on all of the above.

Recent estimates indicate that these students spend from 6.5 to 11 hours per day multitasking on the above activities (Jenkins 2006). They live in a complicated remixed, mashed-up, digital, mobile, always-on media environment. The students function at "twitch speed," thanks to their exposure to video games and MTV. They listen to music on their PCs, Macs, iPods, Zunes, Zens, iPhones, RAZRs, and BlackBerrys. Their experience with the technology has enabled them to master complex tasks and make decisions rapidly (Prensky 2006). Classroom exercises need to extend the capabilities they already possess.

In contrast to these digital natives, teachers are referred to as *digital immigrants*. They still have one foot in the past, and "digital" is their second language, which they continue to learn—and sometimes struggle with—on the fly. For example, immigrants may still print out an e-mail, print a document to edit it, or phone someone to see if he or she received their e-mail. Can you believe that? Is that you? I know. Me too.

Tools for the Classroom

This topic is almost a no-brainer given what students can do with the technology. For small-group or class-size activities, music can be played on a CD player or boom box or PC with portable speakers, or an iPod or MP3 player can be inserted into a speaker system. On a more sophisticated level, music clips can be inserted into PowerPoint slides on a PC or Mac, with audio output from the sound system in the room—if a teacher gets very lucky. There are a variety of configurations; if a teacher runs into difficulty, his or her students will be able to find a way to play the music.

Selecting Appropriate Music

Choosing music for classroom use involves several issues. This section provides guidelines for teachers in the following areas: (1) criteria for selection, (2) types of music, and (3) sources for selecting music. After this section, it'll be time to consider ten techniques for integrating music into teaching.

Criteria for Selection

The lyrics of some of the pop music to which children are listening, especially hip-hop and rap, are out of control in terms of inappropriate language and offensive content. If music is going to be used as a teaching tool, criteria must be established for what is appropriate and acceptable in a teaching-learning context. Each teacher should set his or her own standards for music, just as standards may have already been set for other types of classroom behaviors, such as offensive humor (Berk 2002, 2003), inappropriate or disparaging comments, and issues of civility.

There are two sets of criteria that must be considered: (1) the students' characteristics, and (2) the offensiveness of the lyrics. The first set of criteria relates to salient sociodemographic characteristics: age or grade level, gender, ethnicity, and language-dominance. Teachers know their students, and these characteristics are a must consideration in choosing the right music. The second set of criteria concerns the possible offensiveness of the lyrics: profanity; obscenity; put-downs or ridicule of females, racial and ethnic groups, professions, politicians, and celebrities; and other offensive content.

Clear standards for "acceptable" music should be delineated. The music is being used to facilitate learning, not impede it. A student who is offended by a music clip will withdraw, turn off, and harbor anger, which are emotions hardly appropriate for learning. What is interpreted as offensive is a very personal decision by each student based on his or

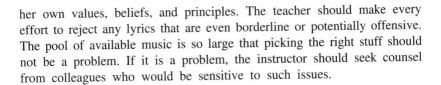

her own values, beliefs, and principles. The teacher should make every effort to reject any lyrics that are even borderline or potentially offensive. The pool of available music is so large that picking the right stuff should not be a problem. If it is a problem, the instructor should seek counsel from colleagues who would be sensitive to such issues.

Types of Music

There are a variety of music types that can be used in the classroom. The actual choice will depend on the characteristics of the students and their interests. The sources identified in the next section will suggest methods for obtaining that information. In the meantime, here is a shopping list to keep in mind: (1) classical; (2) early romantic; (3) late romantic; (4) twentieth century; (5) TV, movie, and Broadway soundtracks; (6) pop (e.g., Top 40, country, easy listening, rap, hip-hop, rock, rhythm and blues); (7) jazz; and (8) new age (Millbower 2000). Other factors to consider—such as emotional effects, visual imagery, and instrumental versus lyrics—are briefly discussed next.

Emotional effects. All of these types can evoke or induce anger, excitement, activity, motivation, love, laughter, whimsy, tears, dreams, calmness, relaxation, sleep, and a coma. Music can have powerful emotional effects. Teachers need to decide the effect they want to produce in a given learning situation. Applied inappropriately, the music can distract and decrease learning, even incite students to riot. Unless rioting is a specific learning outcome, teachers should be very discerning in their choices.

Visual imagery. The emotional arousal evoked by music may also be accompanied by visual imagery. There is an individualized jukebox full of memories inside every one of us. Hearing a piece of music automatically brings those special memories into focus like a photograph (digital, of course). Hearing the music alone triggers a response similar to what has been called a "flashbulb memory" (Brown and Kulik 1977; Sierra and Berrios 1999; Winograd and Neisser 1992).

Music serves as a retrieval cue for those personal memories. When the teacher presses the "play" button, the students' mental picture buttons are pressed into action. Snapshot images suddenly pop into their minds. These images may provide recollections of any of the following: (a) the person performing the song or composition; (b) the person with whom the student associates a scene from a particular TV program, movie, or musical; (c) the person with whom the student heard it; or (d) the time and place where the student heard it. Other details may be recalled as well. All of this occurs in a nanosecond. This image creates feelings, emotions, and moods related to that previous experience. They may be positive (joyous, romantic, humorous) or negative (anxious, discomforting, very painful). Teachers need to be sensitive to the possible negative effects of music that some students might exhibit and handle them appropriately. This is essentially music-induced nostalgia, for better or worse.

Instrumental vs. lyrics. The form of music used in the studies cited previously was predominantly classical. It served as the background to reading, mathematics, and other activities. The slow-tempo selections set a classroom mood and tone that transcended cognitive learning blocks that students' may have experienced. It reached into deeper alpha-wave states to relax students and create a nonthreatening, safe environment to absorb information into long-term memory and foster creativity (Millbower 2000). The fast-tempo pieces snapped their minds to attention and maintained it in betaland. In all of these applications of music, it is the right hemisphere that is called into action. The instrumental selections can be played before class and throughout the day to systematically orchestrate learning activities. The specific techniques will be described shortly.

When music with lyrics is introduced, both hemispheres and the interaction between them are engaged with even greater learning potential than with instrumentals alone. Lyrics add to the familiarity of the music, its meaning and depth, and its overall impact. They can increase memory by association with the content or they can be rewritten to become the content itself. Words synchronized with music are easier to learn than words by themselves. Have you ever sung songs in school (or privately in your own room or shower) to help remember material you were taught? I bet it helped.

When choosing music for class, the specific outcome to be achieved should guide that choice. There are twenty outcomes listed at the beginning of this chapter. For each outcome and technique for using the music, two key questions must be addressed: (1) Do the students need to identify the title of the song for it to work? and (2) How do the lyrics match the content? For some outcomes, the title of an instrumental selection may not be pertinent, such as in the classical pieces referred to in the research. In other cases, it is essential for the song's value to be realized; all students must recognize the song title to make the intended connection with the context.

When lyrics are included, they must relate to the content and context within which they are played; otherwise, they may come across as pointless. Teachers may observe a lot of puzzled looks on the students' faces. Songs with lyrics are obviously more restrictive than instrumental music. The lyrics must have an instructional point. An alternative method is to write new lyrics derived from the actual content. That strategy can be a powerful learning tool. The title of a song with or without lyrics can also be changed to put a relevant spin on the song. The new title alone can have a significant impact on learning and memory.

Sources for Selecting Music

Music selected for classes across the K–12 curriculum is not the same as music chosen for a school's music program. The purposes are very different. Music for the former consists of clips with which most if not all students in the class should be familiar; in the case of the latter, the intent is usually to acquaint students with music forms with which they are most likely unfamiliar. The sections that follow cover published sources and Web sites, identification of music in the students' world, formal student surveys, and CD versus Internet.

Published sources and Web sites. There are several music sources that provide inventories of various types of music for classroom teachers. These sources include books by Andersen, Marsh, and Harvey (1999), Brewer (1995, 2007), Brewer and Campbell (1992), Campbell (1992, 1997, 2000), and Millbower (2000). The Brewer and Millbower books even match the musical selections to the recommended methods for using them. Furthermore, there is a Web site called "Songs for Teaching: Using Music to Promote Learning" (http://www.songsforteaching.com), which contains thousands of pages of lyrics, sound clips, CDs, and downloads of music, cataloged by educational subject and grade level, along with teaching tips, songbooks, and sheet music. Also, see Berk (2002) for other Internet sources.

Identification of music in the students' world. Despite all of these available sources, the primary underpinning for the music techniques that follow shortly is to pick music the students recognize, with which they are familiar and in which they have an interest. Therein lies the connection between their world and the content teachers need to cover. Teachers are not teaching them new music. The aforementioned books do not consider that criterion for the music that is included.

Where does one find music in the students' world? The answer to that question leads us to our second multiple-choice item:

2. What is the most appropriate source from which to select music for class?

   A. *TV program theme* music based on Nielsen Media Research survey results for the specific age group

   B. *Movie* music based on cult classics, Oscar winners, and most recent and popular flicks

C. *Pop* music based on Top 40, including hip-hop, rap (Be Careful!), and R & B

D. *Broadway* music based on shows performed in schools and *High School Musical, High School Musical 2*, and *Camp*

E. Informal and formal student surveys of what music they prefer

F. All of the above

Formal student surveys. Let's chat about choice E for a few sentences. This choice means that teachers should ask their students. Talk to them at every opportunity to find out the latest and most popular music to which they are listening. Furthermore, teachers should conduct formal surveys of their students at the beginning of the first class in the fall and spring semesters, which will furnish a wealth of music information. Each one can be completed in less than ten minutes. Here are eight steps to follow:

1. Pass out two 3" x 5" cards to each student.

2. Have students number each side of each card in the upper right corner with 1, 2, 3, 4, and 5. (Kidding about 5. A little index-card humor.)

3. On side 1, have them list their *three favorite TV programs.*

4. On side 2, have them list their *three favorite movies* seen over the past 3–6 months.

5. On side 3, have them list their *three favorite Broadway shows.*

6. On side 4, have them list their *three favorite pop songs.*

7. Have students pass the 1-2 card to the right and the 3-4 card to the left.

8. Collect all of the cards. (Of course, they will be all mixed up in the wrong piles.)

Now the teacher can collate, compile, categorize, compute, and identify the music to which their students are listening. He or she should take side one and create a frequency distribution of the top ten TV programs the students are watching. A distribution should then be computed for each of the other three sides. Those distributions will yield four top-ten lists that can serve as the pool of music from which clips can be extracted for the entire semester. That pool provides sources from which the teacher can draw TV music themes, hit music from movies and Broadway shows, and pop music with which most of the students will be familiar. That's more than forty different music sources. This is probably the *most accurate inventory of musical selections* a teacher can use.

CD vs. Internet. There are two principal sources from which to obtain music: original CDs or the Internet. There are several factors to consider in using these sources. If the music needs to be extracted and converted to a format compatible with Microsoft's PowerPoint (PP), the Internet may already have the converted version; otherwise, the teacher will have to do the extracting and conversion with specific software, such as Sony Sound Forge Audio Studio 8 or 9, unless he or she has a Mac. Other factors include the following:

Factor	*CD*	*Internet*
Cost	Expensive	Free or cheap
Quality	High	Good–High
Format	Not PP compatible	Some PP compatible
Most recent music availability	Very good	Very good
Related music	Excellent	Not available

Ten Generic Techniques for Using Music in Teaching

There are several resources to consider for specific methods of using music in the classroom and examples of music for those methods. Books by Brewer (1995, 2007), Brewer and Campbell (1992), Campbell (1992), and Millbower (2000) are very useful starting points, and were mentioned previously as sources of music. The music lists are extremely helpful to guide the choice of appropriate music for the method and intended outcome.

Since a teacher's choice of music and specific techniques for using it are contingent on the students' characteristics and musical interests as well as the content to which they are applied, the methods described here are somewhat different than those in the references cited above. The history for the development of those techniques is also very different. Over the past decade, I developed a bunch of methods for incorporating music into one of the most universally hated subjects on this planet: statistics. Just saying the name of the subject conjures up the sound of the "shower" music from *Psycho* along with mental images of the butcher knife and curtain. On the first class of the semester, my students are usually thinking, "Why don't you just kill me now?"

As the foregoing sections revealed, music can be a powerful teaching tool, but it has an untapped potential. Classroom practices using music in a wide range of subjects and courses have to be implemented and tested. The paucity of research evidence cited previously is inadequate to argue wholeheartedly for the positive instructional effects of music, Mozart or otherwise, but maybe we can argue halfheartedly. This is a nontrivial challenge for teachers in order to meet the needs of the Net Geners in their world of music.

The ten generic strategies described next are derived from ten years of practice and research on their effectiveness (Berk 2001, 2002). Two studies were conducted: (1) a survey of 385 students in two undergraduate and five graduate statistics courses over two and a half years was administered to evaluate forty musical selections, and (2) a survey of 232 students in one undergraduate and three graduate courses was distributed to determine whether twelve music pieces in combination with class demonstrations helped students learn the material.

The first survey requested the students to rate the effectiveness of the music to (1) grab their attention and focus, (2) increase their interest in the topic, (3) relax or reduce their anxiety/stress on the topic, and (4) make learning the topic fun. The median ratings for the music were "Extremely Effective" or "Very Effective" for all four outcomes. According to the students, the music significantly increased their level of engagement, helped them relax or reduce anxiety, and made learning fun.

The second survey asked students to weigh in on the music-demonstrations' ability to (1) facilitate their understanding of the statistic, (2) help them remember the statistical concept or process, and (3) help them learn the statistic when they applied it. The research reviewed in earlier sections also examined understanding and memory, although this design was a self-report rather than experimental. Here the students' median ratings for all twelve selections were "Very Effective." Overall, 86 percent or more of each class felt the music-demos improved their understanding, memory, and learning of the statistics.

Based on these studies, the ten highest-rated strategies for using music in teaching are presented here. They are applicable to any subject matter and grade level. Hopefully, future research on their effectiveness in K–12 classrooms will furnish evidence of their usefulness as teaching tools.

1. Prelude to Class and Class Opening Tune-Ups

As students are settling in with their backpacks, coats, and snowshoes and the teacher is preparing for class, background music can be played to set the tone and mood for the day. It can be up- or slow-tempo, depending on the day and the desired effect. It should be played for 1.5 to 5 minutes. The music provides a break in the typical "chatter" noise that occurs as students settle down. It also permits them to check their mental baggage at the door, unwind, relax, or get an emotional boost before class begins.

When the music stops, class begins. Students should be told that that is the cue to end talking and shift gears into learning mode. (*Note:* In the elementary grades, this strategy may be repeated every time the students enter the room from lunch, recess, physical education, or field trips to New York to see *Mary Poppins.*)

Once students are ready, different music may be used to begin the day. For example, the recording of the first violin revving up an orchestra to open a show or concert can be played. This can be followed by a PowerPoint slide of a curtain being raised (transition "uncover" up) to the up-tempo "Everything's Coming Up Roses" or "That's Entertainment," which will engage all of their hemispheres in the room.

2. Opening Day Blockbusters

At the beginning of the school year or semester or after a long holiday break or the teacher's sabbatical, an opening blockbuster should be prepared. The first class, in particular, is critical. From a student's perspective, it can be the forecast of a smash hit or a flop year. It is their first face-to-face impression of the teacher, the content, how he or she teaches, course requirements, expectations, and clothing styles, which are frequently highly predictive of the rest of the year. Since the students do not expect any fireworks, any effort to jump-start their minds and hearts for learning will be appreciated. The blockbuster is also an effective strategy to reduce anxiety, stress, and tension in subject areas that students absolutely dread.

One type of blockbuster is a parody of a popular TV program, movie, or Broadway show with which all of the students are familiar. A parody has both music and humor to which the students can relate. If the parody can be linked to the content in some way, it will be even more meaningful. A well-written and executed parody is a powerful method to kick off anything. Although it may require only a minute of class time to present, the impact can be memorable and perhaps unforgettable. Here are a few thoughts:

> *Gourd of the Dance: A Halloween Treat*
> *Harry Potter Gets Lasik*
> *Indiana Jones and His Angioplasty*
> *Meal or No Meal*
> *Mission: Improbable*
> *Phantom of the Opera Meets Jack Bauer*
> *Card Bored: The Net Generation*

Students watch parodies regularly on TV, on YouTube, and in the movies. Teachers should make every effort to involve students in the planning and execution of the production, which is limited only by the teacher's imagination and creativity. The teacher is the writer, director, and choreographer, as well as the scene, lighting, sound, and costume designer (Berk 2002). It's all in the preparation. The TV programs, movies, and Broadway shows from a teacher's top-ten student survey are fair game for class parodies. Instructors can get ideas from the following lists of parodies. Most of the TV programs are on Comedy Central and many of the movies are cult classics.

TV Programs	Movies	Broadway Musicals
The Daily Show	*Scary Movie I–IV*	*The Producers*
The Colbert Report	*Austin Powers*	*Young Frankenstein*
Reno 911!	*Airplane!*	*Spamalot*
MAD TV	*Scream I–IV*	*Avenue Q*
SNL	*Fatal Instinct*	*Forbidden Broadway*
Chappelle's Show	*Not Another Teen Movie*	
Mind of Mencia	*Young Frankenstein*	
South Park	*The Producers*	
Scrubs	*Blazing Saddles*	
youtube.com	*Monty Python and the Holy Grail*	

3. Topic Introductions

One of the most attention-grabbing, tone-setting, anxiety-reducing strategies to segue from one topic to the next is to play music with a topic slide. The music can be instrumental or with lyrics, but must be related to the content of the topic. Here are a few instrumental examples from our world:

Topic	Music
*Math*terpiece Theatre: LOOOOOONG DIVISION	Theme from *Masterpiece Theatre*
Law 101: "Make My Day!"	Theme from *Law & Order*
Korean War	Theme from *M*A*S*H*
Writing a Coherent Paragraph: Just When You Thought It Was Safe to Go to English!	Theme from *Jaws*
Today's class is brought to you by the no. 15 and the letter M	Theme from *Sesame Street*

Music with a topic slide is the simplest method to incorporate music for a topic introduction. Costumes and props can also be added, such as a smoking jacket and a calabash pipe for *Masterpiece Theatre*, to exaggerate the effect as the music is playing. Four other strategies are the parody mentioned above and content grabbers, class demonstrations, and collaborative learning productions described in techniques 4, 5, and 6, respectively. These theatrical alternatives draw on at least four intelligences, in addition to musical/rhythmic, and can serve as the anchor for how the topic is subsequently covered. The next three sections will suggest a few ideas with examples of how they can be executed.

4. Content Grabbers

Carrying the preceding technique one step further, music can be integrated into the content material being covered, which will be totally unexpected. The right music can pump life into the most boring content. Teachers should not stop with the topic introduction, but build on that music to add other selections as the content is being revealed. They should search for every content nook and cranny to insert up-tempo music. Costumes and props can also accompany this music to provide a visual treat to dramatize the effect. This will keep the students' attention, interest, motivation, engagement, concentration, and emotions in the content rather than drifting elsewhere. Here are a few suggestions with music from our world:

Content	*Music*
Relationships	Theme from *The Odd Couple*
Support Networks	"You've Gotta Have Friends"
Classroom "Survivor": The Good, the Bad, and It Could Get Ugly!	Theme from *The Good, the Bad, and the Ugly*
The Heart	"Simply Irresistible"

5. Introductions to Class Demonstrations

A visual demonstration of a concept, theory, or process can be a powerful vehicle for learning. It requires students to see the process, solve the problem, or critique the encounter. Students will use higher-order thinking skills plus verbal, quantitative, visual/spatial, bodily/kinesthetic, intrapersonal, and interpersonal intelligences, depending on the demonstration. When the "Not-Ready-for-Classtime Players" are called into duty, the demonstration becomes instructional CPR or a defibrillator to resuscitate a dead topic or pump life into boring content.

The demonstration involves transforming a verbal or quantitative concept or process into a visual image. The techniques a teacher can use borrow heavily from the experience and craft of theater (Diamond and Christensen 2005; Millbower 2003; Patterson, McKenna-Cook, and Swick 2006; Spolin 1986; Timpson et al. 1997). Imagine what it would be like to sit in the students' seats and see through their eyeballs how their classmates act out an equation, a poem, or a chemical reaction.

"So where's the music and musical/rhythmic intelligence?" Wait. It's coming. The effectiveness of the demonstration hinges on the students' level of engagement. There are four stages to maximize that engagement: (1) pre-demo setup, (2) grabbing the students' attention, (3) seeing or walking through the demo, and (4) post-demo Q & A follow-up. Let's focus on stage 2. The other stages with examples are described elsewhere (Berk 2001, 2002).

Stage 2 involves the music, which serves as the hook to grab the students' attention and prime their minds, cognitively and emotionally, for the demonstration. Both hemispheres are engaged. When the music stops playing, the students should be on the edge of their seats in anticipation of the demo.

Here's the procedure:

1. Preselect one or two groups each of 4–6 students by gender a few classes before the demo is scheduled. The groups should be equal in size.

2. Tell the students exactly what will happen: The girls will be asked to line up in the back of the room and start walking to the front when the music begins. They will line up across the front; then the boys will do the same. That's it.

3. On the day of the demo, the class is given a serious setup for the demo (stage 1).

4. The first group of students is told to "Get ready." The girls go to the back and line up. The music begins and they walk to the front.

5. Say: "Where are my boys? Get ready." The music begins and they walk to the front.

So what's the big deal? The MUSIC! Here are a few music choices:

Boys	***Girls***
"Bad Boys" (Theme from *Cops*)	"What a Feeling" (*Flashdance*)
"Gonna Fly Now" (Theme from *Rocky*)	"She's a Lady" (Tom Jones)
"Bad" (Michael Jackson)	"I Enjoy Being a Girl"
"Born to Be Wild" (*Steppenwolf*)	(*Flower Drum Song*)
"Law & Order" (Theme)	"Friends" (Bette Midler)
"Stayin' Alive" (*Saturday Night Fever*)	"All That Jazz" (*Chicago*)
	"Dreamgirls" (*Dreamgirls*)

Think about those songs for a moment, all of which are played with lyrics except "Gonna Fly Now" and "Law & Order." Remember, this musical event occurs in English, mathematics, science, history, and every other subject where it doesn't belong. What happens is totally unpredictable. As the students walk to the front, they may dance, box, use hand and arm gestures, or mimic the lyrics. Anything's possible. Sometimes costumes, such as hooded sweatshirts for Rocky or white gloves for "All That Jazz," may be used to exaggerate the effect.

The music and the students' antics become the punchline. It is unexpected by the class. The students erupt with laughter. It takes about 15 seconds for each group to get to the front of the room. Sometimes they'll end with a hilarious group pose. Those 30 seconds create an amazing effect, one which the students will long remember.

When the music stops and everyone settles down, the attention of the class is riveted on the visual demo. What a powerful supercharged opening this music can create, instead of students just walking to the front of the room.

Despite the preparation involved behind the scenes to create the demonstration, the execution by the teacher consists of just pressing the "play" and "stop" buttons on whatever player is being used. The element of surprise is also an essential ingredient in the success of the demonstration. The class never knows when the next one will occur. The students involved in the demonstration are sworn to secrecy. If the demos are sprinkled throughout an entire semester, usually above-average attendance can be ensured. Intermittent reinforcement does work. If a student misses a demo on an important concept or process, there will be no repeat performance.

6. Insertions into Collaborative Learning Productions

Once the teacher presents a parody or demonstration that involves groups of students, it's time for him or her to take one step back and assign students the creation of the production. Based on a basic theater model applied to collaborative learning, groups of five students can be given different concepts or processes to role-play the following:

1. *Director:* guides everyone to focus on a content principle, concept, or process to develop a skit/parody/demonstration with or without a script

2. *Designer:* creates scenery, costumes, props, lighting, sound, music, videos, and games

3. *Technician:* determines equipment, tools, and resources to execute skit/parody/demo

4. *Writer:* prepares script, if required, and sequence of steps to execute skit/parody/demo

5. *Actor(s):* perform skit/parody/demo

This production team will flesh out the visual image it wants to create using the following teaching tools: music, videos, sound effects, games, props, costumes, lighting, sets, and movement. The demonstration can be scripted or unscripted following the rules of improvisation (Berk and Trieber, in press; James and Williams 1981; Newton 1998). A maximum time limit should be imposed. A 10-minute block is usually adequate. When the final product is performed to illustrate a principle, concept, or process, it will be an unforgettable experience for the team, the performers, and the entire class.

This collaborative learning activity matches the technology-savvy, kinesthetic, experiential, participatory, team-oriented characteristics of the Net Geners and their cultural world (Berk 2008; Prensky 2006). Moreover, it instructionally draws on at least five of their multiple intelligences; their leadership, artistic, technical, and musical gifts; and their learning styles, while fostering deep learning.

The teacher should meet with each group to monitor ideas and progress. Most of the work should be done outside of class. He or she can also make suggestions or assist with technical support, such as the music and videos, or the students can produce their own. Similar to the class demonstration directed by the teacher, this student production engages everyone in the preparation and possibly everyone in the live performance. Here the music is only one requirement. The choice of music and videos must be approved by the teacher.

7. Class Activity Background Interludes

Anytime students are requested to write or type an assignment in class requiring anywhere from 30 seconds to 3 minutes, the time frame presents another opportunity for music. What happens when students are writing answers to one or two questions, writing a minute paper on the three most important points just covered, or solving a problem or case? What do you hear? NOTHING! Dead silence. It's like morgue time on *CSI*.

Background music can be played to help students relax and drift into alphaland or to produce a chuckle or two in betaworld. The music chosen is critical. The goal is not to distract but to facilitate the activity so that students are more insightful, reflective, accurate, and creative in their responses than they would be without the music. Low-tempo selections might include classical music or "The Rainbow Connection" (*The Muppet Movie*); up-tempo, chuckle-inducing music could be themes from *Jeopardy!*, *Sesame Street*, and other favorite TV shows. The music should be related to the activity and timed with the length of the activity. When the 3-minute music piece is over, the work stops and papers are collected. This use of music should be planned carefully and implemented occasionally with the element of surprise, similar to all of the preceding techniques.

8. Test Reviews with Games

There are so many games, but so little time. Students love games, especially video games. I'm not sure teachers can produce video games in class, although some students probably can (see Prensky 2006). Popular TV games, however, are a real possibility. The games can be used to teach material and review content for a test. The music theme and game-background slides available on the Internet make it even more authentic and exciting to play than a board game.

The most widely used games adapted to teaching are *Deal or No Deal*, *Who Wants to Be a Millionaire*, *Hollywood Squares*, and *Jeopardy!* The template slides allow teachers to supply their own content (see http://qbx6.ltu.edu/natsci/games.shtml). Other games can also be used, but the identifiable theme music is a must to provide an instant connection with students.

9. Postreview Pep Rally

After conducting a test review, the teacher should hold a pep rally in or out of the classroom to get students pumped up and motivated to do their best on the test, just like it was the day before a football or basketball game. Why should sports events get all of the attention and hype? Why not academic events like tests and projects?

Once the review is completed and before the students leave, the teacher should ask if there are any remaining questions. He or she should then give a few words of encouragement, make the expectations clear for the test performance, and offer up "We Are the Champions" (Queen), "We Will Rock You" (Queen), "Hakuna Matata" (*Lion King*), the high school football fight song, or some other up-tempo, appropriate music. Students should depart with the proper supportive tone and the feeling that the teacher really cares about their performance. In this application, the teacher creates the context; the music sets the tone.

10. Posttest Pick-Me-Ups

After test or project results have been posted or handed back to students, the teacher should comment on the class's performance, placing each score or grade in the context of the rest of the assessments. If some of the students are disappointed with their performance, the teacher should tell them: "Think about the words to this song" (and press "play"). Here are a few suggestions:

"Tomorrow" (*Annie*)

"Don't Worry, Be Happy" (Bobby McFerrin)

"What a Wonderful World" (Louis Armstrong)

"Happiness" (*You're a Good Man, Charlie Brown*)

The above selections always produce a few smiles. The music says something positive to all students—especially to those who didn't do as well as they had expected. It can change the tone and attitude of students faster than anything the teacher could possibly say, except maybe "That F doesn't count."

Finale

This chapter was designed to acquaint you with the potential value and uses of music across the K–12 curriculum. Music is a virtually untapped resource for teaching the Net Generation and for drawing on their multiple intelligences to increase the success of every student. Its learning potential was expressed as twenty instructional outcomes at the outset and ten specific techniques at the end. The material in between those anchors was mostly research filler. The theory and research on the brain and music and learning were reviewed and critiqued. The research on music and learning was more encouraging than informative. The results accumulated so far are merely suggestive rather than conclusive. A considerable amount of research evidence needs to be collected in all subjects and grade levels.

The technology requirements and the sources for selecting appropriate music were also described. However, when applying the Olympic judging criteria of "technical merit" and "artistic impression" to the instructional uses of music, it seemed that the technical aspects were the easiest to implement. It's the artistic side that is the most challenging; the effectiveness of the music depends on the teacher's creativity, imagination, and artistic gifts, which will inevitably make the greatest difference in the classroom. Those gifts, moreover, must be accompanied by systematic planning and preparation, which is very time consuming.

I challenge all teachers to seriously consider the ideas presented in the foregoing pages along with the lists of available resources for music to add a dimension to their teaching that will change their classroom approach forever. Once they incorporate music into all that they do, their view of teaching and their students will never be the same. In the years to come, maybe students will request CD soundtracks of their classes to download onto their iPods, iPhones, and MP3 players rather than the movies they've watched. Then they can play and relive those magical teaching moments with music. Wouldn't that be a shift?

References

Adaman, J. E., and P. H. Blaney. 1995. The effects of musical mood induction on creativity. *Journal of Creative Behavior* 29 (2): 95–108.

Andersen, O., M. Marsh, and A. Harvey. 1999. *Learn with the classics: Using music to study smart at any age.* San Francisco: LIND Institute.

Berk, R. A. 2001. Using music with demonstrations to trigger laughter and facilitate learning in multiple intelligences. *Journal on Excellence in College Teaching* 12 (1): 97–107.

———. 2002. *Humor as an instructional defibrillator: Evidence-based techniques in teaching and assessment.* Sterling, VA: Stylus.

———. 2003. *Professors are from Mars®, Students are from Snickers®: How to write and deliver humor in the classroom and in professional presentations.* Sterling, VA: Stylus.

———. 2008. Star tech: The net generation. In *Teacher education yearbook XVI: Imagining a renaissance in teacher education,* ed. C. C. Craig and L. F. Deretchin. Lanham, MD: R & L Education.

Berk, R. A., and R. H. Trieber. In press. Whose classroom is it anyway? Improvisation as a teaching tool. *Journal on Excellence in College Teaching.*

Bever, T., & R. Chiarello. 1974. Cerebral dominance in musicians and non-musicians. *Science* 185:537–39.

Brewer, C. B. 1995. *Music and learning: Seven ways to use music in the classroom.* Tequesta, FL: LifeSounds.

———. 2007. *Soundtracks for learning: Using music in the classroom.* Bethel, CT: Crown House.

Brewer, C. B., and D. G. Campbell. 1992. *Rhythms of learning: Creative tools for developing lifelong learning.* Tucson, AZ: Zephyr Press.

Brown, R. 1986. Suggestive-accelerative learning and teaching in special education. *Journal of the Society for Accelerative Learning and Teaching* 11 (1): 13–22.

Brown, R., and J. Kulik. 1977. Flashbulb memories. *Cognition* 5:73–99.

Butzlaff, R. 2000. Can music be used to teach reading? *Journal of Aesthetic Education* 34 (3-4): 167–78.

Campbell, D. G. 1992. *100 ways to improve teaching using your voice and music: Pathways to accelerate learning.* Tucson, AZ: Zephyr Press.

———. 1997. *The Mozart effect: Tapping the power of music to heal the body, strengthen the mind, and unlock the creative spirit.* New York: Avon Press.

———. 2000. *The Mozart effect for children: Awakening your child's mind, health, and creativity with music.* New York: Avon Press.

Chabris, C. F. 1999. Prelude or requiem for the "Mozart effect"? *Nature* 400:826–27.

Davidson, C. W., and L. A. Powell. 1986. Effects of easy-listening background music on the on task performance of fifth-grade children. *Journal of Educational Research* 80 (1): 29–33.

Diamond, M. R., and M. H. Christensen. 2005. Bravo! Do acting games promote learning in the college classroom? *Journal on Excellence in College Teaching* 16:55–67.

Douglas, S., and P. Willatts. 1994. The relationship between musical ability and literacy skills. *Journal of Research on Reading* 17 (2): 99–107.

Fisch, S. M., and R. T. Truglio, eds. 2001. *"G" is for growing: Thirty years of research on children and Sesame Street.* Mahwah, NJ: Erlbaum Associates.

Furnham, A., and A. Bradley. 1997. Music while you work: The differential distraction of background music on the cognitive test performance of introverts and extroverts. *Applied Cognitive Psychology* 11:445–55.

Gardiner, M. F., A. Fox, D. Jeffrey, and F. Knowles. 1996. Learning improved by arts training. *Nature* 381:284.

Gardner, H. 1983. *Frames of mind: The theory of multiple intelligences.* New York: Basic Books.

———. 1993. *Multiple intelligences: The theory in practice.* New York: Basic Books.

———. 1999. *Intelligence reframed: Multiple intelligences for the 21st century.* New York: Basic Books.

———. May 2005. *Multiple lenses on the mind.* Paper presented at the ExpoGestion Conference, Bogota, Colombia.

Gardner, H., and T. Hatch. 1989. Multiple intelligences go to school: Educational implications of the theory of multiple intelligences. *Educational Researcher* 18 (8): 4–9.

Gazzaniga, M. 1992. *Nature's mind.* New York: Basic Books.

Goleman, D. 1998. *Working with emotional intelligence.* New York: Bantam Books.

Graziano, A. B., M. Peterson, and G. L. Shaw. 1999. Enhanced learning of proportional math through music training and spatial-temporal training. *Neurological Research* 21:139–52.

Hallum, S., and C. Godwin. September 2000. *The effects of background music on primary school pupils' performance on a writing task.* Paper presented at the annual conference of the British Educational Research Association, University of Wales, Cardiff.

Hallum, S., and J. Price. 1998. Can the use of background music improve the behaviour and academic performance of children with emotional and behavioural difficulties? *British Journal of Special Education* 25 (2): 88–91.

Hébert, S., and I. Peretz. 1997. Recognition of music in long-term memory: Are melodic and temporal patterns equal partners? *Memory and Cognition* 25:518–33.

Hetland, L. 2000. Learning to make music enhances spatial reasoning. *Journal of Aesthetic Education* 34 (3-4): 179–238.

Ho, Y., M. Cheung, and A. S. Chan. 2003. Music training improves verbal but not visual memory: Cross-sectional and longitudinal explorations in children. *Neuropsychology* 17 (3): 439–50.

James, R., and P. Williams. 1981. *A guide to improvisation: A handbook for teachers.* Oxon, England: Kemble Press.

Jenkins, H. 2006. *Convergence culture: Where old and new media collide.* New York: New York University Press.

Jourdain, R. 1997. *Music, the brain, and ecstasy: How music captures our imagination.* New York: Avon Press.

Kenealy, P., and A. Monseth. 1994. Music and IQ tests. *Psychologist* 7:346.

Lamb, S. J., and A. H. Gregory. 1993. The relationship between music and reading in beginning readers. *Educational Psychology* 13:19–26.

Leng, X., and G. L. Shaw. 1991. Toward a neural theory of higher brain functioning music as a window. *Concepts in Neuroscience* 2:229–58.

Lozanov, G. 1978. *Suggestology and outlines of suggestopedy.* London: Gordon & Breach.

MacLean, P. 1990. *The triune brain in evolution.* New York: Plenum.

Marks-Tarlow, T. 1995. *Creativity inside out: Learning through multiple intelligences.* Reading, MA: Addison-Wesley.

McKelvie, P., and J. Low. 2002. Listening to Mozart does not improve children's spatial ability: Final curtains for the Mozart effect. *British Journal of Developmental Psychology* 20:241–58.

Millbower, L. 2000. *Training with a beat: The teaching power of music.* Sterling, VA: Stylus.

———. 2003. *Show biz training.* New York: American Management Association (AMACOM).

Miller, L., and M. Schyb. 1989. Facilitation and interference by background music. *Journal of Music Therapy* 26 (1): 42–54.

Miller, M. 1997. *Brain styles: Change your life without changing who you are.* New York: Simon and Schuster.

Mohanty, B., and A. Hejmadi. 1992. Effects of intervention training on some cognitive abilities of preschool children. *Psychological Studies* 37:31–37.

Mullikin, C. N., and W. A. Henk. 1985. Using music as background for reading: An exploratory study. *Journal of Reading* 28 (4): 353–58.

Nantais, K. M., and E. G. Schellenberg. 1999. The Mozart effect: An artifact of preference. *Psychological Science* 10 (4): 370–73.

Newman, J., J. H. Rosenbach, K. L. Burns, B. C. Latimer, H. R. Matocha, and E. R. Vogt. 1995. An experimental test of "the Mozart effect": Does listening to his music improve spatial ability? *Perceptual and Motor Skills* 81:1379–87.

Newton, B. 1998. *Improvisation: Use what you know—make up what you don't! Improvisation activities for the classroom.* Scottsdale, AZ: Gifted Psychology Press.

North, A.C., and D. J. Hargreaves. 1997. Liking, arousal potential, and the emotions expressed by music. *Scandinavian Journal of Psychiatry* 38:45–53.

Overy, K. 2003. Dyslexia and music: From timing deficits to musical intervention. *New York Academy of Sciences* 999:497–505.

Patterson, J., D. McKenna-Cook, and M. Swick. 2006. *Theatre in the secondary school classroom: Methods and strategies for the beginning teacher.* Portsmouth, NH: Heinemann Drama.

Polk, M., and A. Kertesz. 1993. Music and language in degenerative disease of the brain. *Brain and Cognition* 22 (1): 98–117.

Prensky, M. 2006. *"Don't bother me mom—I'm learning."* St. Paul, MN: Paragon House.

Rauscher, F. H., and S. C. Hinton. 2006. The Mozart effect: Music listening is not music instruction. *Educational Psychologist* 41 (4): 233–38.

Rauscher, F. H., G. L. Shaw, and K. N. Ky. 1993. Music and spatial task performance. *Nature* 365:611.

———. 1995. Listening to Mozart enhances spatial-temporal reasoning: Towards a neurophysiological basis. *Neuroscience Letters* 185:44–47.

Rauscher, F. H., G. L. Shaw, L. J. Levine, E. L. Wright, W. R. Dennis, and R. L. Newcomb. 1997. Music training causes long term enhancement of preschool children's spatial-temporal reasoning. *Neurological Research* 19:2–8.

Rideout, B. E., and C. M. Laubach. 1996. EEG correlates of enhanced spatial performance following exposure to music. *Perceptual and Motor Skills* 82:427–32.

Rideout, B. E., and J. Taylor. 1997. Enhanced spatial performance following 10 minutes exposure to music: A replication. *Perceptual and Motor Skills* 85:112–14.

Robazza, C., C. Macaluso, and V. D'Urso. 1994. Emotional reactions to music by gender, age, and expertise. *Perceptual and Motor Skills* 79 (2): 939–44.

Sarnthein, J., A. V. Stein, P. Rappelsberger, H. Petsche, F. H. Rauscher, and G. L. Shaw. 1997. Persistent patterns of brain activity: An EEG coherence study of the positive effect of music on spatial-temporal reasoning. *Neurological Research* 19 (2): 107–16.

Schellenberg, E. G., T. Nakata, P. G. Hunter, and S. Tamoto. 2007. Exposure to music and cognitive performance tests of children and adults. *Psychology of Music* 35 (1): 5–19.

Schlaug, G., L. Jancke, Y. Haung, J. Staiger, and H. Steinmetz. 1995. Increased corpus callosum size in musicians. *Neuropsychologia* 33 (8): 1047–55.

Sierra, M., and G. E. Berrios. 1999. Flashbulb memories and other repetitive images: A psychiatric perspective. *Comprehensive Psychiatry* 40 (2): 115–25.

Sousou, S. D. 1997. Effects of melody and lyrics on mood and memory. *Perceptual and Motor Skills* 85:31–40.

Sperry, R. 1973. Lateral specialization of cerebral function in the surgically separated hemispheres. In *The psychophysiology of thinking*, ed. F. McGuigan and R. Schoonover. New York: Academic Press.

Spolin, V. 1986. *Theatre games for the classroom: A teacher's handbook.* Evanston, IL: Northwestern University Press.

Steele, K. M. 2000. Arousal and mood factors in the "Mozart effect." *Perceptual and Motor Skills* 91:188–90.

Steele, K. M., T. N. Ball, and R. Runk. 1997. Listening to Mozart does not enhance backwards digit span performance. *Perceptual and Motor Skills* 84:1179–84.

Steele, K. M., K. E. Bass, and M. D. Crook. 1999. The mystery of the Mozart effect: Failure to replicate. *Psychological Science* 10:366–69.

Stough, C., B. Kerkin, T. Bates, and G. Mangan. 1994. Music and IQ tests. *The Psychologist* 7:253.

Stratton, V., and A. Zalanowski. 1994. Affective impact of music vs. lyrics. *Empirical Studies of the Arts* 12:173–84.

Thompson, W. F., E. G. Schellenberg, and G. Husain. 2001. Arousal, mood, and the Mozart effect. *Psychological Science* 12 (3): 248–51.

Timpson, W. M., S. Burgoyne, C. S. Jones, and W. Jones. 1997. *Teaching and performing*. Madison, WI: Magna Publications.

Vaughn, K. 2000. Music and mathematics: Modest support for the oft-claimed relationship. *Journal of Aesthetic Education* 34 (3-4): 149–66.

Waterhouse, L. (2006a). Inadequate evidence for multiple intelligences, Mozart effect, and emotional intelligence theories. *Educational Psychologist* 41 (4): 247–55.

———. (2006b). Multiple intelligences, the Mozart effect, and emotional intelligence: A critical review. *Educational Psychologist* 41 (4): 207–25.

Williams, W. M., T. Blythe, N. White, J. Li, R. J. Sternberg, and H. Gardner. 1996. *Practical intelligence for school*. New York: HarperCollins College Publishers.

Winograd, E., and U. Neisser, eds. 1992. *Affect and accuracy in recall: Studies of "flashbulb" memories*. New York: Cambridge University Press.

Zull, J. E. 2002. *The art of changing the brain: Enriching the practice of teaching by exploring the biology of learning*. Sterling, VA: Stylus.

⦿ ⦿ ⦿   Technology in Action: The Role Technology Plays in Adult Basic Education, General Educational Development, English as a Second Language, and Workforce Development

Tracy Loken Weber

Introduction

Technology is constantly changing, evolving and prominent in today's global economy and workforce. How does technology play a role in ABE, GED, ESL, and workforce development for today's adult learners? Let's explore where we are today and where technology needs to go in the world of adult literacy, and the role technology currently plays in adult literacy organizations.

Among adults, over 30 percent nationwide and over 27 percent (157,000+) in the city of Milwaukee have low or very low levels of literacy, meaning they cannot read at all or they struggle to read to their children, find an intersection on a map, write a short letter explaining a mistake on a credit card bill, etc. (GMLC 2006).

History of Adult Literacy

With the passage of 1998's Workforce Investment Act, the Adult Education Act—in place for over thirty years—was made obsolete. The National Adult Education Professional Development Consortium provides a history of this landmark piece of legislation on its Web site, an excerpt of which appears below.

> The Federal government has been involved in adult education for well over 200 years. The nature and extent of Federal attention to the needs of adult learners has varied over this period, but,

Tracy Loken Weber is Programs Director for the Milwaukee Achiever Literary Services in Milwaukee, Wisconsin, and a national reviewer for the U.S. Department of Education, serving on the National Commission of Technology and the Future of Teacher Education with the Association of Teachers in Education (ATE).

from its earliest days, the government provided funds to establish, encourage, and expand programs to assist adults in overcoming educational deficiencies, which would hinder productive and responsible participation in the life and growth of the nation.

At the state level, evening schools for adults, part-time education, and citizenship/Americanization classes for the foreign-born and the Chautauqua experience were forerunners of the State/Federal adult education movement. State histories give evidence of organized adult education as early as the 18th century.

However, it was not until the early 1960s, in the Kennedy administration, that poverty and adult literacy became a concern. Building on Kennedy's efforts, President Lyndon Johnson and a sympathetic Congress launched a series of programs to end poverty and increase the role of the Federal government toward the improvement of education. With the passage of the Economic Opportunity Act (August 20, 1964), Title II B of Public Law 88-452 created the first Adult Basic Education program as a state grant. The 1964 Federal legislation established a state and Federal partnership to focus on the most basic of educational skills for adults who had not completed secondary education. Funding for states that first year was $18.6 million. In 1965, 37,991 adults enrolled nationally in what was known as ABE (Adult Basic Education). At times, Federal efforts have been disjointed; sometimes they overlapped with other similar programs. But, throughout the past thirty-four years, there have been continuous programs focused on increasing adult literacy skills through the Adult Education Act.

Literacy and Technology

For adult learners, using a computer means belonging to this day and age. Learning to use a computer is easier than learning to read. Mastering a few computer commands, knowing how to log on to a system, or printing out a copy of your input imparts a feeling of confidence as a learner—that's the beginning. And that beginning must be available to all adult learners, no matter what ethnicity they are, no matter what level they are at, no matter what part of the world they are in.

Technology integration should be used with adult learners as it is used in the workplace. Learning environments need to support the acquisition of lifelong learning skills and the ability of students to cope with constantly changing workplaces (Kotrlik and Redmann 2005). Adult learners need access to word processing for reading and writing, databases for information processing, spreadsheets for number crunching and planning, and graphics to add clarity and extra fun. Telecommunications, computer-assisted design, and desktop publishing are also useful to adult learners. Adult learners realize the importance of computer literacy in addition to literacy programs, and many learners combine both forms of instruction.

The importance of computers in literacy education is clear. However, making decisions about computer hardware and software seems to be among the most difficult for managers of literacy programs. Technology decisions tend to be expensive. Mistakes are costly, and literacy programs have very limited resources. There is also a lack of adequate information, so program directors often feel unsure about choosing hardware or deciding how much of a program's technology resources should be allocated for management and how much for instruction. The newness of the technology precludes anyone having sufficient experience to provide advice about long-term impact. Adult literacy service providers are nonprofit 501(c)(3) organizations that depend on the support of volunteers and receive critical funding through grants, foundations, and donors.

Nonprofit organizations providing adult literacy have found a new technology spot online for up-to-date software at a not-for-profit price. TechSoup.com is helping to bridge the digital divide. Due to TechSoup. com, nonprofit organizations are able to purchase software for adult learners to gain computer literacy skills necessary to be competitive in today's technologically driven economy.

Finally, most software and hardware vendors know little or nothing about adult literacy. It is very difficult for them to understand a literacy program's needs, let alone match those needs to a technological solution.

Technology Integration

Before integrating technology into your literacy program, it is helpful to examine questions and issues concerning your literacy organization and available technology. The focus of these questions is to help you determine how to move your program from where it is now to where you want it to be:

1. What are the current strengths and weaknesses of the adult literacy program?

2. How can technology improve the program? What do you want the technology to do? Is this a one-time purchase or part of a long-range plan?

3. What needs to be done to implement technology into the program—raise funds to purchase equipment? Train tutors? Provide time for learners to use equipment at times other than during the tutoring session?

To begin answering these questions, it is important to take a close look at your organization as well as available technology.

Learner Characteristics

- background experience in and out of learning sessions
- level of achievement
- learning style (preferences vs. genuine strengths and weaknesses)
- individual academic goals

Tutor Characteristics

- tutor comfort with technology
- amount of training time tutors require to feel comfortable with a particular software program
- tutor experience with teaching

Differences in Setting

- use of materials during class time
- use of materials outside of class time
- independent use of materials
- use of materials by pairs of learners
- use of program by tutor and learner

Reading and Writing Software

When nonprofit organizations begin looking for software, they will notice several categories of reading and writing programs:

Computer Literacy

Programs in this group help learners familiarize themselves with the keyboard and improve their typing skills.

Integrating Reading and Writing

This group contains both reading and writing activities.

Word Recognition

These programs are designed to help learners add to their vocabulary and recognize familiar words more quickly.

Reading Comprehension

These programs deal with a variety of reading comprehension skills, including literal comprehension, inferential comprehension, prediction, sequencing events, and analyzing cause-and-effect relationships.

Language Arts

This category contains a variety of programs covering parts of speech, compound words and contractions, and completion of sentences via context clues.

Writing

These programs fall into two categories. The first category emphasizes mechanics of writing and helps learners improve capitalization, punctuation, and spelling skills. The second category emphasizes composition and includes word processing programs and story starters. A variation of this type of software (such as Print Shop and PrintMaster) allows learners to create greeting cards, letterheads, banners, signs, and flyers.

Vocabulary

Software programs in this category are shell programs. Tutors or learners must fill in information before the programs can be used. For example, Discovery Software and CrossWord Magic allow the user to create crossword puzzles.

Public Domain Software

This category typically contains a wide variety of programs, some of which are appropriate for literacy learners trying to improve their reading and writing skills.

Formats of Educational Software

The educational software programs listed above can come in a wide variety of formats:

Drill and Practice

This format is used to reinforce basic, discrete skills in such areas as word recognition, reading comprehension, spelling, grammar, and vocabulary development. Learners can often use this software independently. Being able to use a computer often motivates learners to practice skills usually found boring when presented as pencil-and-paper activities.

Instruction and Drill

This format contains a short instruction section—often one or two screens—at the beginning of a lesson. The remainder of the lesson is drill and practice.

Educational Games

This software involves competition or earning points as well as drill and practice. Games often motivate reluctant learners. Good educational games require learners to spend more time learning than simply moving pieces around a game board.

Tutorials

This type of software is similar to one-on-one instruction. The computer presents information and then asks a series of questions. Learners' answers determine what information the computer will present next.

Strategy Building

This type of software involves going beyond learning content to actual problem solving. Students might learn several strategies for recognizing words in context, such as using context clues, word configuration, and phonics. Or the program might emphasize the importance of prediction in the reading process and give learners practice in this skill.

Authoring

This kind of software is a shell program. Tutors must fill in information before the student can use the program. Some pieces of this software come with a few samples ready to use. Tutors can use these with their learners and then go on to create their own exercises or activities.

Selecting Computer Software

For technology-savvy individuals, the following questions are easily answered. But how would non-technically-minded individuals respond to the following questions in order to make appropriate decisions about what software to use for instruction?

- What hardware and peripherals are necessary to run the program?
- What are the objectives of the program? How will it help learners meet their needs?
- Is the material geared toward the adult age group in content and presentation?
- Is the program based on sound educational principles?
- Does the program allow for student control of presentation sequence and rate when appropriate?
- Does the program allow learners to respond quickly and easily without requiring excessive or unnecessary keyboarding?
- Does the program provide appropriate feedback for both correct and incorrect responses?

o Can learners use the software independently, or must tutors be present to help learners?

o How much time and effort will learners and tutors have to put into learning the program?

All of these lists of features and questions may seem intimidating. In the world of adult literacy, technology is a risky business, but the benefits far outweigh the risks. As one tutor stated recently about the use of computers: "I never thought technology would make such a world of difference to my learner. It's amazing to see how technology is the motivator for learner achievement." With this in mind, it is imperative that adult literacy organizations invest time and limited funding resources toward the future of technology and adult literacy.

Current Role of Technology and Adult Literacy

Adult learners are motivated to learn how to use a computer and the necessary technology that will help advance their personal and professional lives. Technology is currently being utilized in many aspects in adult literacy for those nonprofits that are able to afford it. Nonprofits using technology will find that their adult learners not only have the will to learn but also understand the importance of technology and being able to appropriately apply it in their daily life skills and within the workplace.

As a technology educator, I have made a decision to take a nontraditional approach to the advancement of technology and computer literacy. In the opinions of some of our learners, this has been a welcome change and has made technology "real"—not something that continues to bore them to death.

The traditional model was laid out by Ralph Tyler in 1949 and is generally considered the mainstream way to conceptualize curriculum development (Prevedel 2003). However, this approach—still used by many professional educators in schools across the United States—has created a stigma about how adult learners should be expected to learn in classrooms of twenty-five or more. Large class size is a likely reason why so many students are not successful in our schools today, leading to high dropout rates and reports that nearly 1 in 3 high school students does not graduate (Chaddock 2006).

Adult literacy issues are evident, and the time is now to understand how adult literacy providers can make the learner-driven approach toward basic literacy comprehension and workforce development a reality. Malcolm Knowles, often considered the father of adult education, says that adults come to education "with a life-centered, task-centered, or problem-centered orientation to learning" (Knowles 1984, 12). For the most part, adults do not learn for the sake of learning.

Project-Based Learning and Technology

Project-based learning (PBL) is built on the principle that the "need to know" about a topic drives the development of language and literacy skills, and the desire to tell others engages learners in language work to a much greater extent and results in more time on-task and deeper learning than does conventional class work. Project-based learner-centered orientation puts primary emphasis on participants' involvement with curriculum development processes (i.e., on students setting their own goals, exploring their own experiences, shaping the curriculum, and evaluating their own learning). This participatory approach emphasizes drawing curriculum content from the social context of learners' lives as well as involving them in curriculum development processes (Auerbach 1993).

Adult basic education (ABE) and English as a second language (ESL) teachers have been saying for a long time that our learners have complicated lives and don't have time to do homework, which is true enough. What we find with PBL, however—particularly if there is a student showcase involved—is that most adult learners make the time to meet and prepare their presentations outside of class and often spend an inordinate amount of time working on PowerPoint shows or videos; creating posters, iPod voice projects, comic-book-style writing, personal journals, or photo shows created in iPhoto; or otherwise making sure their presentations meet the standards they have set for themselves. One learner told me: "I tell my husband or my mother-in-law, 'this is like work; I have to meet with my team, and then I tell them about the project so they understand.'"

PBL also owes a great deal to "constructivism"—the notion that the brain makes sense of the world by connecting new information to existing information, and that we as human beings are constantly engaged in creating knowledge (i.e., we don't just passively absorb ideas and store them as we hear them in our brains; rather, all ideas and experiences are processed before they are stored, which explains why two people remember the same event differently). Our minds actively weave together what we hear, read, and see, and the greater our engagement with ideas and the more channels we use to work with these ideas (visual, auditory, print-based, hands-on), the deeper the learning goes. We also know that the more connections the mind can make around a central idea, the more accessible these ideas will be in the future and the longer they will be remembered.

If we then create positive experiences around the development of knowledge and the acquisition of skills and strategies, we begin to create an impetus for lifelong learning, in spite of the fact that the learning process may have been a bit stressful along the way.

PBL, with its focus on investigations, the learning of new technologies, and the nerve-wracking prospect of having to conduct a presentation to "real people" (not just to one's own teacher and classmates), also reflects the notion that language develops in fits and spurts, and that a bit of mild stress is a good thing in that it actually propels us forward in our learning.

This can be a difficult concept to get across, since many teachers try to protect their learners from anxiety and are reluctant to demand anything that might make them uncomfortable. Yet we know from learning theory that very little, if any, new learning happens when we remain in our comfort zone. In order to grow cognitively, we need to take on new challenges and deal with the frustration of not knowing how things will turn out.

If we look back at learning experiences that have stayed with us over the years, as well as the achievements that we were the most proud of, there was probably a fair amount of anxiety involved at one point. It's the same for the learners I've worked with. Before a showcase, they are a mess—their stomachs hurt, they curse their teachers, and they are close to dying of stagefright (not all that different from their teachers, who on a regular basis wonder what they've gotten themselves into).

Yet in the end, adult learners not only survive but get to bask in the glory of having done things no one expects of adult learners, including using computers to create PowerPoint presentations with sound, producing mini-documentaries, creating CDs that amaze their children, and speaking in front of a crowd.

Then, of course, there is the connection to participatory education and to the engaged learning models that good technology supports.

Adult Literacy Technology Projects

Programs

Programs that continue to assist with computer literacy currently include Rosetta Stone, English Tutor, Side by Side Interaction, Focus on Grammar Basics, GED Test Preparation, Learn to Speak English, Mavis Beacon, Atomic Learning, GCFLearnFree.org, Microsoft Office Suite, and numerous Web sites appropriate for adult learning.

Slices of Life

Every year learners in Milwaukee are encouraged to work with their tutor to complete a short essay for the yearly publication *Slices of Life*, a booklet published locally. Learners are thrilled at the thought of seeing their name and works published for the first time in their lives. Learners work diligently with their tutors over many months to convey their thoughts and reasons for why they are pursuing adult education. The end result: hundreds of first-time authors who are proud of their accomplishment and ecstatic to share it with family, friends, and their tutor.

Comic Book

It is important to demonstrate the various types of computers for first-time technology learners. During the first two weeks, learners work on personal computers and become familiar with their assigned computer. During the third week, learners are exposed to the Apple iBook, iMac, and iPod. Their quest for new knowledge and excitement about being able to create their own comic book makes for a wild, hands-on, laughter-filled environment. In this way, learners are having fun while gaining important knowledge, and are openly and actively communicating with each other. As a team, we create a masterpiece from which we produce a comic book for every participant.

iPod

Many adult ESL learners struggle with pronunciation. With that in mind, the integration of the iPod has opened the door for immediate feedback. Learners and their tutors are able to speak into the iTalk connected to the iPod and are able to listen to themselves immediately. There are many podcasts also available for ESL learners to listen to and practice with to help them communicate more clearly with their children.

Digital Video

Projects involve a digital video camera, a speaker, a tripod, and a team of creative learners. This technology creates an environment that moves learning into a new dimension.

- Appearing on video is powerful. A screen presence in front of an audience feels great and means you are somebody to be paid attention to.
- Videotaping allows you to practice and edit what you want to say. We always give the learners the right to say "cut" when they fumble or feel awkward. Those "do-overs" give learners a chance to articulate what they want to say and practice until they feel

comfortable. Often, learners hate to edit their written essays ("I wrote it and you said it was good—I'm done"). They seem to have a much keener ear for language when they listen to themselves and often catch mistakes, awkward phrasing, or sentences that go on and on. Knowing that each person has only a minute or so to talk on tape really encourages learners to think about what they want to say and say it clearly. These are skills that are applicable to workplace communication, GED writing, and discussions on academic topics.

○ Learning how to create a film project has a multiplier effect for learners. Just getting their hands and heads around the technology moves things in a new direction. It can also change the social identity that learners project, as they are now filmmakers, producing knowledge and information for others. They use the same kinds of skills that professionals use—storyboarding, setting scenes, taping, editing, integrating graphics and music, and then going public with their work. For these learners, being a filmmaker (even if their team only does a short "how-to" video on how to change a tire or how to make a romantic dinner) changes their identity from someone who struggles with English or doesn't read well to someone who is a "film producer" (professional titles are used as part of the credits).

PowerPoint

Learner-created videos and PowerPoint presentations can be used in orientation and as a means of broadcasting to the community that a particular literacy program connects learning to the real world and offers skills that count beyond the test. Learners are able to create a PowerPoint presentation that conveys a specific message about a particular subject, such as a sports figure, an artist, a personal hero, a well-loved pet, or even their workplace's production-line assembly.

Our final project was student driven and shown to peers and co-workers, earning them promotions for their stellar work and mastery of technology through the JobLink Workforce Development Computer Literacy Program. Learners excelled, and felt proud about their work in class. The learners made a difference in their educational functioning level, improved their workplace morale, and received promotions at their respective employers—thereby increasing their earned wages and contributions to their family.

Conclusion

Technology is the motivational tool that will afford adult learners endless opportunities in the twenty-first century. The challenge lies within the circle of adult literacy service providers to supply adequate resources and knowledgeable staff and tutors with the ideal skills to apply these learning solutions to their benefit.

Adult learners understand the importance of technology, which also gives them the motivation they need to stay competitive in today's economy. Adult learners must be able to access information through technology: it helps them think critically, solve problems, and communicate as members of a collaborative team. Technology has allowed learners to excel to new heights—proof that the phrase "the sky's the limit" is merely a springboard for today's adult learners to achieve something beyond what was once thought to be unachievable.

References

Auerbach, E. 1993. Putting the P back in participatory. In Adult literacies, special issue, *TESOL Quarterly 27* (3): 543–45.

Chaddock, G. 2006. US high school dropout rate: High, but how high? *Christian Science Monitor.* Retrieved July 1, 2006, from http://www.csmonitor.com/2006/0621/p03s02-ussc.html.

Educational Testing Service. 2007. *America's perfect storm: Three forces changing our nation's future.* Retrieved February 15, 2007, from http://www.ets.org/stormreport.

Eyre, G. 1998. *Federal response to adult illiteracy: A history of the adult education act.* National Adult Education Professional Development Consortium. Retrieved March 10, 2006, from http://www.naepdc.org/issues/AEAHistort.htm.

Greater Milwaukee Literacy Coalition. 2006. *The greater Milwaukee literacy coalition: Literacy through collaboration.*

Knowles, M. 1984. The art and science of helping adults learn. In *Andragogy in Action: Applying Modern Principles of Adult Learning.* San Francisco: Jossey-Bass. Quoted in Prevedel 2003.

Kotrlik, J. W., and D. H. Redmann. 2005. Extent of technology integration in instruction by adult basic education teachers. *Adult Education Quarterly 55* (3): 200–219.

Milheim, K. 2007. Influence of technology on informal learning. *Adult Basic Education and Literacy Journal* 1 (1): 21–26.

Pasnik, S. 2007. iPod in education: The potential for teaching and learning. Retrieved April 3, 2007, from http://www.mages.apple.com/education/ipodpaper/iPod_in_Education_whitepaper.pdf.

Prevedel, A. 2003. Values and beliefs: The world view behind curriculum. *Focus on Basics* 6 (C).

▯ ▯ ▯ Online Learning: A Catalyst for Change

Jamey Fitzpatrick

This paper discusses the work of the Michigan Virtual University® (MVU®) and outlines several factors that are influencing the adoption and growth of online learning in public education. MVU will celebrate its tenth year in operation in 2008. As a private nonprofit 501(c)(3) organization, MVU was created by the state of Michigan to serve as a champion for online learning. In the early days, MVU focused on workforce development needs and served as a catalyst for change, working closely with higher education institutions.

Today, MVU operates one of the largest virtual schools in the United States. Since its inception in 2000, the Michigan Virtual School™ (MVS™) has given over 40,000 young people the opportunity to take an online course in everything from Mandarin Chinese to oceanography to forensic science. MVU also operates Michigan LearnPort®, an online professional development portal that gives Michigan's K–12 community—teachers, administrators, school-bus drivers, food-service workers—an opportunity to access online professional development.

National Graduation Rates

According to current research, only 70 percent of students are graduating from U.S. high schools each year. That number—which has held steady for a number of years—is unacceptable. Something needs to be done to address this national crisis. We need to take a closer look at this policy challenge and begin to explore new and innovative approaches to delivering educational services to teenagers. Both recognizing that about a third of our nation's students are not graduating from high school and knowing the negative employment outlook for high school dropouts should be a big motivator for state and local policy leaders to think about innovation and change.

Jamey Fitzpatrick is President and CEO of Michigan Virtual University, a private non-profit 501(c)(3) corporation.

According to *The Silent Epidemic*—a report funded by the Gates Foundation—half of those students who drop out of high school indicate that their classes are not interesting (Bridgeland, Dilulio Jr., and Morison 2006). This should come as no surprise to most educators and parents. When students are asked to use one word to describe their high schools, they typically don't respond with words like *exciting, engaging*, or *fun*. Too many young people think that high school is boring—especially the students who are dropping out.

Tensions within the K–12 Community

Five major factors are beginning to converge, forcing the public education system to explore new delivery options such as online learning. These factors are described below.

1. Time Constraints

Prisoners of Time—a report published in 1994 by the National Education Commission on Time and Learning—is as relevant today as it was when it was first published. The report looks at the relationship between time and learning, focusing on how much core academic learning can actually be forced into a school day. In order to think beyond the parameters of a six-hour-per-day learning environment, we need to think about how we can exploit and harness the power of technology to engage students after school, in the evenings, on the weekends, and during the summers and other breaks during the year. The school calendar may be the most difficult paradigm to change in public education, and online learning may be the easiest way to shift this paradigm.

2. Budget Limitations

Like most other publicly funded social services, K–12 education struggles with adequate funding levels on an annual basis. As state budget revenues decline or experience limited growth, funding for K–12 education becomes even more difficult. Funding is not a new challenge for public education, and some argue that adding options for student choice, such as charter schools, weakens core support for schools. Budget constraints will likely continue to plague the K–12 community for the foreseeable future. At the high school level, this trend will impact the breadth and depth of curricular offerings available to students, especially in rural and urban schools. Online learning programs may represent a cost-effective strategy for expanding curricular options for students, especially for low incidence courses.

3. Relevance

Increasingly, students struggle to see how classroom instruction relates to their world outside of school. Great teachers work every day to make learning relevant so that students can understand the connection between what happens in the classroom and its importance to their future. Making instruction relevant has become especially difficult as more students use technology outside of school. Significant opportunities exist to use technology-based resources to make teaching more connected to the world of work and students' personal lives. Most students who take online courses enjoy using the technology and communicating with teachers in the same way they communicate with their family and friends outside of school.

4. Web 2.0 Tools

In the early days of the Internet, most people were only consumers of online information. Today, with the introduction of wikis, blogs, video-sharing Web sites, social networking services, and other Web 2.0 tools, more people are also producers of online information. For obvious security and student safety issues, many of these tools have not been widely adopted at the K–12 level. Increasingly, student expectations will begin to drive the usage of these innovative communication tools. Educators will need significant professional development to better understand how these tools can be used to impact teaching and learning in meaningful ways.

5. Globalization

In *The World Is Flat*—a book primarily focused on how commerce in the world has changed as a result of technology—Thomas Friedman tells the story of a small-business owner evaluating his fast-food business (2005). The owner determined that his drive-up window service was an area of low customer satisfaction with high error rates. As a result, he decided to invest in an Internet connection and video camera, and outsourced the window's operations to a call center in Colorado. The call center was staffed by a group of women who had been highly trained in telephone skills. Through the video camera and microphone, they were able to take customer orders and instantaneously send them to the kitchen. The process was so effective that the workers in the kitchen couldn't tell that the order was issued from the call center in Colorado. Within three months, the business owner saw his error rates completely fall off and his sales actually increase.

If you can outsource a drive-up window service at a fast-food restaurant, then organizations can outsource just about any service, including education. When we think about globalization in Michigan, we inevitably think about losing automobile manufacturing jobs. The possibility of outsourcing educational service is scary to most people in the United States. However, the use of online learning will continue to globalize instruction in this country and elsewhere. Michigan Virtual School has a cadre of online teachers scattered all over the state of Michigan who teach online part-time. Most of these educators are full-time classroom teachers in public schools. Policy leaders need to begin to explore how the use of the Internet will give them access to high-quality teaching resources not available in their local community. Teaching world languages online will likely become the first academic area to fully explore online global education solutions. MVS provides Mandarin Chinese language courses online through a unique partnership with the Confucius Institute at Michigan State University (MSU). The online instructors for these courses are native speakers from China who are enrolled in graduate programs at MSU.

National Trends in Online Learning

Online learning is becoming more common throughout the United States at all levels of education. Last year, it is estimated that over one million K–12 students and approximately 3.5 million college students took an online course. In most states, student and parent demand for online learning at the K–12 level is not being adequately supported. The amount of public support for state-sponsored virtual schools varies, and most states are struggling to develop a funding mechanism that is predictable and stable, and that can accommodate future growth.

There are currently many common misperceptions about online learning. One idea espoused by critics is that it signals a depersonalizing of education. The experiences gained by MVS instructors suggest just the opposite. They claim it is easier to personalize the classroom and differentiate instruction because of the significant one-on-one communications in online classes. Many MVS instructors indicate that they get to know their virtual students better than the students in their regular classrooms. Technology is changing human communication in unpredictable ways, and we need to figure out how to harness this tool to benefit teaching and learning.

An interesting phenomenon is happening in the United States compared to around the globe in terms of online learning for K–12 education. In the United States, we are using online learning primarily as a supplemental resource rather than as a reform strategy. In Singapore, they close their schools for one week and migrate all their learning online for that period. This strategy forces teachers to be prepared—they deal with a lot of natural disasters in Singapore, and also want to be prepared in the event of a bird flu pandemic that shuts down schools for a month or longer. So Singapore is looking at online learning as a reform strategy, as are countries like China and India.

Michigan's Policy on Online Learning

In 2006, the Michigan legislature passed a law that revamped the state's high school graduation requirements. One of the requirements included in the new law is that students take an online course or have a meaningful online learning experience prior to graduation. This experience can be met in one of three ways: (1) they can take an online course from an online provider like MVS, a community college, or a local school district; (2) they can have an online learning experience of at least twenty hours in duration; or (3) they can have an online learning experience embedded in each of the sixteen courses that make up the new Michigan Merit Curriculum—the core courses that every student must take.

Today's students need to know how to use the technology, but their experiences using technology tend to be focused on recreational and entertainment applications. Most students do not use technology for significant formal learning activities. Michigan's new online learning requirement will provide all students with an opportunity to learn how to learn in a technology-rich environment.

Conclusion

Public education is serving a different group of students today than it did fifteen or twenty years ago, and there's a gap between how young people live outside of school and how they are expected to live and work inside of a classroom environment. To a large extent, this gap is related to the use of technology, and unfortunately that gap is getting wider, causing more of our young people to feel disengaged with our public education system.

Whether you want to lose twenty-five pounds, learn how to cook a French dessert, make a shirt out of duct tape—whatever it is that you have a personal goal for—you can go online and find other people around the globe who have a similar interest. The Internet is aggregating geographically dispersed individuals with common interests and learning needs. Obviously, this expands the learning economy. Some refer to this as the democratization of learning. For others, it's a scary idea because it brings up traditional turf issues.

The latest numbers from the Pew Foundation suggest that as of late 2004, about 87 percent of teens use the Internet on a daily basis (2005). According to Everett Rogers's Innovation Adoption Curve, successful innovation takes time (2003). We are in the early stages of the online learning movement for the K–12 community. In the next ten to fifteen years, this technology will become more mature, and our comfort level with it will increase. The K–12 education system in the United States has much to gain from the adoption and use of Internet-based instruction that provides alternative pathways to learning and matches student interests.

References

Bridgeland, J. M., J. J. DiIulio Jr., and K. B. Morison. 2006. *The silent epidemic: Perspectives of high school dropouts.* Gates Foundation.

Friedman, T. 2005. *The world is flat: A brief history of the twenty-first century.* New York: Farrar, Straus and Giroux.

KnowledgeWorks Foundation and the Institute for the Future. 2006–2016 Map of future forces affecting education. www.kwfdn.org/map/map.aspx.

National Education Commission on Time and Learning. 1994. *Prisoners of time.* Washington, DC: U.S. Government Printing Office.

Pew Internet & American Life Project. 2005. Protecting teens online. www.pewinternet.org/PPF/r/152/report_display.asp.

Rogers, E. M. 2003. *Diffusion of innovations.* 5th ed. New York: Free Press.

⬤ ⬤ ⬤ Looking to the Future: A Legislative Perspective

Sandy Kress

Technology in the Age of NCLB

I have been active in public law and policy in the education arena for the last twenty or so years at the local, state, and federal levels, culminating in the work done in 1999, 2000, and 2001 on the reauthorization of the Elementary and Secondary Education Act (ESEA)—No Child Left Behind. It was quite an experience in terms of bringing the likes of Senator Kennedy and George W. Bush together, but one that made an impression on me. It's always worth reflecting on the simple idea of what it takes to bring people from different sides together. How do we find ways to do more "and" as opposed to "either/or," "my way," or "your way"? This is a very important issue generally and in terms of the current challenges facing us with regard to technology. All the issues that will be raised—How do we get the funding? What is the technology to be used for? How do we know we're successful?—need to be resolved in a win-win manner. A win-win environment is the best time to get increases in spending to pay for the kinds of changes that we need to make. We need to keep that in mind as we look forward to the next round of changes in law and policy in Washington and in the states as well.

Analyzing Where Our Students Are

There's currently a real interest in putting substantial additional resources into better data. What do I mean by "better data"? One important component would be to break down assessments and understand what they mean—for the school as well as for the student. One of the great flaws in education today is that we don't have—at least at all the levels where it would be useful—a sophisticated analysis of the strengths and weaknesses of each student. Individual students are all over the map in terms of strengths, weaknesses, learning styles, deficiencies. Doctors can examine us, taking into consideration literally thousands of factors in our

Sandy Kress is Partner at Akin, Gump, Strauss, Hauer & Feld, LLP.

body, and make a determination, and yet we seem to be unable to have a discussion with the relevant players—the teacher, the administrator, the school system, the parents—about exactly where Johnny is. There's been a lot of talk recently about attributing the high dropout rate to student boredom, but I believe the true culprit is the years of accumulated neglect toward the problems of our young people and a failure to address them adequately. Through the surveying that I have done, I found that boredom is largely a function of the real problem—or at least the real surface problem—which is that some ninth and tenth graders are actually two, three, and even four years behind in terms of the level of work they can do. Now boredom may have contributed to them being behind in the first place, but the inadequacies to which there's been a lack of attention given have caused an accumulative deficiency, leading to an inability to perform altogether. However jazzy the teacher's presentation, however much technology is available, it's very hard to perform tenth grade work when you're reading at a sixth grade level. Therefore, for the future of our young people, it is very important that we understand exactly where students are year to year, and we can use new technology and data systems to gather that kind of knowledge.

There have been some exciting applications entering the field since 2000, including handheld devices that not only allow a teacher to do an assessment almost instantaneously but also record that assessment. That data can then be used both for accountability purposes and—more importantly—for getting an understanding of where a student is and in what areas that student needs help, which is vital in terms of structuring appropriate interventions. Data can also be helpful in terms of bringing about an understanding of the differentiation of treatments that are needed not only for the school but for the student. We've got to bring our data capabilities in education up to the standards of the twenty-first century, just as has been done in other industries and endeavors.

Aligning Learning to the Standards

The second area in which technology poses a plethora of opportunities is in its ability to both deliver education in a way that is interesting, exciting, and accessible to students, and to align that education more effectively with the standards that have been developed in both the state and the district. Sure, technology can be fun—my children use it in all kinds of ways, many of which enhance their knowledge base—but when technology can be used to better deliver to the standards that the state expects, then it serves not only local and state purposes but the purposes called for in No Child Left Behind. Many of the computer-based programs being developed today are amazingly compact, yet they provide students' access to a variety of resources—particularly video, faculty presentations, opportunities for interaction, news clips—which gives them different ways of seeing the data and the history behind what they're learning. This kind of efficient learning reminds me of when I was studying for the bar. During law school, the knowledge seemed extremely wide ranging—I could barely get my arms around it. But when I was studying for the bar, somehow all of the critical knowledge came. Now this is not to say that I shouldn't have gone through the process of the Socratic method, but in terms of understanding the key content—the way it related to each other, some of the important lessons of it—I ended up learning at the end of the process how compact it all was. The amazing thing about technology is that it allows us in very exciting ways to compress the core learning that is actually called for in the standards.

Now why is that important? One, it's important because it allows young people to get the knowledge and skills that are required by the standards in a way that works, in a way they like, and in a timely fashion. By doing so, it means we've met the obligations of No Child Left Behind and state accountability laws and the need to get young people to master the knowledge and skills that the adults in the state have said are important. But guess what else? It also frees up the teacher and the students to spend time on other things—to round out their education, to go deeper into subjects, to study all of those things that the anti-accountability people say are being crowded out of education; in essence, it affords us the opportunity to get to "and." This business today of "either/or" is devastating. Either we're going to study grammar or we're going to study poetry; either we're going to be punitive or we're going to be loving and caring and supportive; either we're going to have accountability or we're not. One of the wonderful things about technology is its power to get us to "and."

It's a fact that students need to learn to the standards. That may seem schoolmarmish of me to say, but I have been working for some time with a college readiness commission in Texas, and make no mistake about it—colleges expect students to master the fundamentals in the four core areas. So again it's not a matter of "either/or." They're going to be expected both to do the rock climbing and to walk up the steps. As part of our work, we did focus groups among people in business and higher education all across the state of Texas, and it amazed me how it was always "and." No one ever said—the businesspeople included—that the traditional kinds of knowledge taught in schools were unimportant in the twenty-first century. They are important, but students also need critical-thinking, analytical, and problem-solving skills. The focus-group participants never said "when push comes to shove"; they never said "either/or." Technology allows us the ability to think "and."

Offering Differentiated Learning

The third important thing about technology in this standards-based environment is that it allows us to offer more differentiated learning, with a focus on educating students who are in different places—and most of them are these days. There are many students who are behind and who need the very best kind of intervention, and for those students, technology can help. There are many students who are gifted, who aren't going to do well with some purely standard or common-denominator type of presentation; technology is helpful for them, as well. I've seen programs developed in the last ten years—approved by the What Works Clearinghouse—that are remarkable at getting young people up to algebra proficiency, people who are behind and are able to use the technology to move ahead. I've seen a program created by a technology company in Richardson, Texas, that found a way to use technology for professional development as well as to accelerate learning. Technology is a very clear solution to some of the issues and challenges of No Child Left Behind in the standards-based movement.

The Future of NCLB

It's very hard to say what direction we're going to take in terms of No Child Left Behind. There's currently a lot of reaction and counterreaction, different sides overplaying their hands. We're in a murky place, and the common view seems to be that we ought to wait till the election of a new president to decide. Unfortunately, however, there's been far less discussion of education in this campaign than there was in 2000. Perhaps this is because the issue's become so hot—meaning we're at a stage where things are so controversial and have been made so political that politicians would rather talk about anything else. This is not a good thing for the long term and for the kind of support and clear policy we need. If this is the case, I hope that Secretary Spellings will spend the next year working to achieve a better implementation of No Child Left Behind so that the tools it was intended to generate are more apparent, and the obstacles, problems, and labels that I think have morphed from the law will be less significant. This would create a better environment for policymakers and for us moving into the next step.

Make no mistake about it, the standards-based reform movement has worked. In 1990, results of the National Assessment of Educational Progress (NAEP) showed that 85 percent of African American fourth graders were below basic in math. This was right at the beginning of the standards-based reform movement, following the first President Bush's domestic summit on education in Charlottesville in 1989, attended by the nation's governors. This was about the time the states started looking at standards, testing, and consequences in a fairly crude way. Texas, North Carolina, and Massachusetts came on board in 1993, followed by other states, but in 1990, the movement was just starting. As of the 2007 test, the percentage—while still too high—was reduced to 35 percent. That means that more than half of the African American fourth graders who were below basic in 1990 are now at or above basic. The numbers at proficiency or above are still way too low, but they've gone from virtually zero up to the double digits on a test administered on a level playing field. (There is no teaching to this test; it's a national test administered through a survey.) This is the same for Hispanics. White students and Asian students have shown a steady increase at the same time. The problem with all this happy data is that it's improvement from a very low place—nowhere near college readiness—and the gains don't continue into the high schools. This leads me to the idea that there needs to be emphasis in the reauthorization on the "S" of ESEA—on secondary education and spending time on goals directed toward college and job readiness, which I think will also be part of the debate in Washington. There's a tremendous resistance that has settled in, largely through opposition from the National Education Association (NEA) and other groups. The Democrats are torn. Many civil rights groups are rallying to the law. Newspaper editorialists are watching all of this, turning surprisingly pro-NCLB. Yet some Republicans are moving back to their old stance of no funding, no federal involvement. It's very complicated and convoluted, and it's going to affect all of us as we move forward.

Conclusion

We cannot just look at technology as a good thing to do—on its own, separate from the world of education law and policy in which we live. If we continue to use it because it's fun or because it's new or because it tends to work a little bit better than something else, rather than tie it into meeting these other key objectives, it will never play out, and we will not benefit from the power of these tools as much as we can and should.

As leaders in education, we must do what we can—whether it's in the classroom, in the school, or through policy—to drive elected officials and policymakers toward the notion of "and" as opposed to "either/or." We need to begin to see the world in the same way as does the principal of UT Elementary School—a charter school in East Austin, supported by the University of Texas—in whose school all poor African American and Hispanic students were rated exemplary by the state. Principal Ramona

Treviño proudly stated that her school met the efficiency, results, and objectives of No Child Left Behind, while creating a loving and caring environment for both teachers and students that meets their social and other needs as well. If we can use technology to help us shift to "and," we will be doing better by our young people in helping them be successful.

⬮ ⬮ ⬮ Rethinking the Structure of High Schools in South Texas: An Early College Collaboration

Dee Hopkins

The evolution of education in America—specifically the evolution of its public high schools—has been an ongoing process, a process that many individuals feel has not stayed current with the demands of our global world. Bill Gates, for instance, thinks our high schools are obsolete. He told participants of the 2005 National Governors Association that even when high schools were working the way they were designed, they did not teach today's young adults what they need to know to live in tomorrow's world. "Training the workforce of tomorrow within the high schools of today is like trying to teach kids about today's computers on a 50-year-old mainframe. It's the wrong tool for the times" (Gates 2005).

Many would agree with Gates. Our country has yet to recognize that we no longer live in an agrarian society, that the majority of our students in public education are no longer Anglo, that English is not the home language for many students, and that a high school diploma is no longer sufficient to obtain a job that will support a family. And yet our educators and politicians are reluctant to change the paradigm.

Our Ailing Public High School System

Those of us within higher education recognize the shortcomings of today's high school diploma. Many students finish their junior year with all their high school requirements fulfilled, goof off during their senior year so that they can graduate with their class, and then come to the university needing remedial work. Other students never obtain sufficient reading, writing, or mathematical proficiency to succeed in college. Both groups have forced colleges and universities to create developmental classes—which essentially amounts to expensive duplication of high school instruction with no college credit.

Dr. Dee Hopkins is Dean of the College of Education at Texas A&M University—Corpus Christi in Corpus Christi, Texas. As of July 1, 2008, Dr. Hopkins will be the Dean of the College of Human Resources and Education at West Virginia University.

Many students drop out of high school. The nationwide rate for black high school dropouts is twice that of whites, and the number of Hispanics dropping out is even greater. The numbers themselves are astounding. During the 2003–2004 school year, 42,979 of students in Texas did not finish the twelfth grade. For those states reporting nationwide, the total was 545,266 (Texas Education Agency 2005). Statistics show that only 40 percent of high school dropouts have jobs. What's more, they are nearly four times more likely to be arrested than their friends who stayed in high school. In addition, high school dropouts are far more likely to give birth to children in their teens, and one in four will turn to welfare or other kinds of government assistance (Bridgeland, DiIulio Jr., and Morison 2006).

The makeup of students in America's high schools has changed. The western states have the largest influx of new populations—including those from Mexico and Central American countries, as well as those resulting from increasing emigration from the Orient. (We may need to erect a new Statue of Liberty, a sister for our western shores.) Today over 40 percent of the young people in our public schools are not white. The largest growth has been the Hispanic population, but other groups—including African American and Asian/Pacific Islanders—are also increasing. The white population continues to decline; in 1972, 78 percent of public school attendees were white; in 2005, that number had dropped to 58 percent. The populations increasing most rapidly are also the populations attending some of our high-poverty schools. Forty-nine percent of Hispanics, 48 percent of African Americans, and 36 percent of Native Americans are in schools with the highest measure of poverty (U.S. Department of Education 2007).

High school curriculum is trailing as well; students are not receiving the international knowledge and skills necessary to access the good jobs of the future. Today only 50 percent of American high school students study a language, and for 70 percent of them it is one year of introductory Spanish. Critical languages—Arabic, Korean, Farsi, and Mandarin Chinese—are for the most part unavailable. In the countries that speak those languages, however, students learn English along with their own language. A recent Rand Corporation survey of sixteen global corporations found that when they compared universities around the world, U.S. students were seen to be "strong technically" but "shortchanged" in cross-cultural experience and "linguistically deprived" (Stewart 2007).

Public Education's Challenge

Our challenge is to redesign America's high schools to make sure our students gain the knowledge and skills they need to succeed in this global age. That means a rigorous curriculum designed to give students—all students—the scientific and technological literacy necessary for tomorrow's economy. It must also provide them with the cross-cultural leadership skills they will need to exist in a demographically diverse environment. Most importantly, students must learn how to adapt to rapid change.

Texas has been an active participant in many initiatives seeking to improve high schools, including the American Diploma Project Network. It was the first state to adopt a college-ready curriculum as its default curriculum for all students. The state also revised its state assessments to more carefully match the knowledge and skills students should have in high school and on through graduation. Texas has moved exit-level assessment from tenth grade to eleventh grade to more accurately assess student achievement in high school. In 2003, the state, led by Governor Rick Perry and other elected officials, invested in the Texas High School Project (THSP)—a public-private partnership. The goals of the THSP were to boost graduation rates and to increase the number of high school students prepared for postsecondary success. Dedicated funds from the state in the amount of $148 million in appropriated and federal funding, combined with the contributions of several philanthropic partners, including the Bill & Melinda Gates Foundation, the Michael & Susan Dell Foundation, the Wallace Foundation, National Instruments, and the Communities Foundation of Texas, resulted in a $260 million collaboration dedicated to improving Texas high schools.

Creating an Early College High School

One outcome of this alliance is the University Preparatory High School, a collaboration between Texas A&M University–Corpus Christi (TAMUCC) and Flour Bluff Independent School District (ISD). In 2004, the Gates Foundation, through the THSP, approached us to see if we would consider establishing an early college high school. Knowing the challenges many of our high schools faced and recognizing the need for a new high-school model, we accepted. A $400,000 grant ($100,000 per year for four years) from the Gates and Dell foundations was used for planning and the initial establishment of the school. Criteria required that the school be autonomous; that it remain small, with no more than one hundred students per grade level; and that student selection give priority to first-generation college attendees, representatives of underrepresented peoples,

English language learners, and members of low socioeconomic families. These students are in abundance in South Texas, and they need assistance entering higher education.

Conceptually, an early college high school blends high school and college into a coherent educational program designed so that all students can complete up to two years of college while still in high school and working toward a high school diploma. Skills for preparing students for college course work begin in the middle schools, with emphasis placed on reading, writing, mathematics, science, and computer literacy. This seamless transition from K–12 education to the university allows students to begin their college work when their performance shows that they are ready.

When we accepted the challenge to create an early college high school, we were one of thirteen doing so in Texas. There are now plans to increase that number to thirty in the coming year. Each of the current thirteen is unique. Several are partnerships between community colleges and independent school districts. Some are located in urban areas; others in rural settings. Some, like Collegiate High School—another early college partnership in our community between Del Mar Community College and Corpus Christi ISD—place high school freshmen in core college courses immediately. These schools hope to award sixty-hour associate degrees, along with high school diplomas when students graduate. Others, like University Prep, delay the full-time integration of students on the university campus, focusing first on college-readiness skills at the high school. At the university, less emphasis is placed on an associate's degree, with more emphasis placed on doing well in core classes.

The Fundamentals of University Preparatory High School

Instead of reading, 'riting, and 'rithmetic, University Prep has adopted Bill Gates's new three R's as the basic building blocks of better high schools: relevant course work; rigorous course work; and meaningful relationships between teachers, administrators, and university professors and students and parents. During the first two years, the high school teachers focus on college preparation. Courses are blocked, assigned readings are intensified, and writing is required in all classes. In addition, everyone takes computer, math, and science courses.

Ninth graders are acclimated to the university campus by regular visits to hear speakers, attend sporting events, and enjoy theater and musical performances. All of their course work is preparatory high school work; no university classes are taken by high school freshmen.

Tenth graders also visit the university campus on a regular basis. In addition, they participate in university core course work (three classes each semester), which is taught at University Prep by university professors. At the eleventh and twelfth grade level, students attend classes at the university almost full time and take core courses along with other undergraduates. A primary difference between University Prep students and university undergraduates is the staff support they receive simultaneously at the high school.

University Prep is a school where everyone believes that obtaining a college education is possible. From the moment students begin as freshmen, the goal they are given is to obtain a college degree. They are not selected for the school because they have the highest grades, because they are gifted, or because they can afford a special preparatory school experience; they are selected because they want to succeed—and now success means a college degree.

Benefits and Outcomes

The benefits to University Preparatory High School students—and their parents—are immense. For most, a college education was not previously part of their dream—too expensive to consider and too far from their frame of reference to attempt. Now, students like Lisa, a beautician's daughter, has the opportunity to have the first two years of college paid for and completed before she graduates from high school. Bright, Hispanic, and the child of a single parent, Lisa cannot wait to get to school each day.

Raul, also Hispanic, worried that he would miss playing sports. At University Prep, he is allowed to select only two extracurricular activities. Now a sophomore, Raul likes being on the baseball team, but has not had time to miss football, basketball, and soccer.

The university and the school district also benefit from this collaboration. Flour Bluff ISD continues to receive payment from the state for each child attending school. The district then uses a portion of those funds to pay the university tuition for each child at University Prep. TAMUCC does not, however, require University Prep students to pay designated tuition, only board-authorized tuition. Special fees are also adjusted on a "when needed" basis so that freshmen pay no extra fees, and sophomores pay only for library privileges and identification cards. Once they are enrolled in university classes, University Prep students are included in the undergraduate count at TAMUCC. The credit hours they generate each semester increases the formula funding the university receives. In addition, once the school is fully operational, the university will be assured of one hundred new students every year—all members of the underrepresented groups TAMUCC is charged to serve. Gates Foundation funding did what it was intended to do—it got us up and running. Now, however, working together, the ISD and the university are making it possible for University Preparatory High School to continue without outside funding.

Less visible but more long-lasting benefits of University Preparatory High School include the research opportunities afforded TAMUCC faculty and students. A senior faculty member has already launched a longitudinal study of students attending the school. She and her doctoral students hope to have qualitative data regarding the long-term experiences and opinions of these early college attendees. Although it is early, hopes are high that a large majority of the students attending University Prep will go on to college—and will graduate.

Although University Preparatory is only in its second year, we are already seeing some noteworthy results: 99 percent of students passed the Texas Assessment of Knowledge and Skills (TAKS) reading test at the end of their freshman year; 30 percent of students achieved "commended performance" on the TAKS reading test; and 74 percent of students passed the TAKS mathematics test, in a year where the statewide passing average was 60 percent (J. Crenshaw, pers. comm.).

Already visible is the emergence of a college-bound culture. Students are more willing to do outside reading and homework. They are aware of their own deficiencies and are working to eliminate them. The focus for everyone in the school is the common goal of college readiness.

Also apparent is the benefit of a small school environment. With a maximum of one hundred students per level, relationships are strong. Every teacher is familiar with every student. Parents are more involved and keep in contact with the school. When students took the Texas Higher Education Assessment (THEA) for the first time, parents called immediately to see how they could help their children raise their scores. This is the state test University Prep students will need to pass before they will be admitted to a university. Another heartening factor is the retention of students in the program. During the first year, only four students left University Prep—two because their families moved out of the district, and two because they wished to return to a regular high school environment. Most noteworthy, in the first year of operation, only five disciplinary referrals were made. The collaboration between teachers, administration, and parents is strong, and it is affecting the students—both their performance and their behavior.

Although it is early, every indication points to University Preparatory High School's success. It eliminates the lost senior year, encourages an early commitment to attend college, offers a close environment with personalized instruction, emphasizes academics rather than activities, eases the adjustment to a college campus, provides up to sixty hours of college course work for minimal cost, and gives students a two-year head start toward obtaining a college degree. University Prep's establishment has not been easy, and there have been numerous roadblocks. In spite of the pitfalls, the passion and belief of those involved in this innovative high school design are energizing others to take a look at new curriculum, new structures, and new ways of educating the citizens of tomorrow.

Conclusion

In closing, I want to share an observation Calvin of the *Calvin & Hobbes* comic strip makes regarding education. Entering his classroom, he says,

> Today for Show and Tell I've brought a tiny marvel of nature: a single snowflake. I think we might all learn a lesson from how this utterly unique and exquisite crystal . . . turns into an ordinary, boring molecule of water just like every other one, when you bring it into the classroom.

Taking Calvin's words to heart, University Preparatory High School is a new design for secondary education—one that recognizes every child as utterly unique.

References

Achieve, Inc., and the National Governors Association. 2005. An action agenda for improving America's high schools. National Education Summit on High Schools. Retrieved November 5, 2007, from http://www.nga.org/portal/site/nga/menuitem.1f41d49be2d3d33eacdcbeeb501010a0/?vgnextoid=da97739a87165110VgnVCM1000001a01010aRCRD.

American Diploma Project Network. Texas action plan for the American Diploma Project Network. 2006. Retrieved October 24, 2007, from http://www.achieve.org/files/TX-ADPplan.pdf.

Bridgeland, J. M., J. J. DiIulio Jr., and K. B. Morison. March 2006. The silent epidemic: Perspectives of high school dropouts (Civic Enterprises in association with Peter D. Hart Research Associates). Retrieved October 20, 2007, from http://www.civicenterprises.net/pdfs/thesilentepidemic3-06.pdf.

Gates, B. 2005, February 26. Prepared remarks. Speech given at the National Education Summit on High Schools. Retrieved November 6, 2007, from www.gatesfoundation.org/MediaCenter/Speeches/Co-chairSpeeches/BillgSpeeches/BGSpeechNGA-050226.htm.

Stewart, V. 2007. Putting the world into world-class education: Innovations and opportunities. Speech given at the 2007 CADREI conference in Sedona, Arizona.

Texas Education Agency. 2005. Secondary school completion and dropouts in Texas public schools 2003–2004. Retrieved October 20, 2007, from http://www.tea.state.tx.us/research/pdfs/dropcomp_2003-04.pdf.

U.S. Department of Education. 2005. Common core of data. Retrieved October 22, 2007, from http://nces.ed.gov/ccd.

———. 2007. Status and trends in the education of racial and ethnic minorities. Retrieved October 20, 2007, from http://nces.ed.gov/pubs2007/minoritytrends/index.asp.

Vander Ark, Tom. 2005. Rethinking our education system [Electronic version]. *Business Perspectives*. 13, 3. Article retrieved October 23, 2007, from http://www.amazon.com/Rethinking-Our-Education-System-Perspectives/dp/B0008I6KGC/ref=sr_1_3/105-2232057-48980 15?ie=UTF8&s=books&qid=1194368036&sr=1-3.

ⓞ ⓞ ⓞ Preparing Educators Through Online Program Delivery

John E. Jacobson

As a young aspiring teacher going through a teacher preparation program in the early 1970s, I remember my mentor telling me that to be an effective teacher, I must learn all I can about my students. That solid and sage advice has not changed over the years and truly applies to all who teach. As we guide teacher candidates through our various preparation programs, we must learn all we can about them—their strengths, needs, learning styles, and so forth. We are told that teachers who are being prepared today come from a generational group called the "millennials"— and so we must ask ourselves, What traits define this group?

According to Alicia Moore (2007), millennials are much more diverse than the members of any other generation. They're pressured to perform, they're ambitious, and they're achievers. They're team oriented, though in a different way than how we've traditionally conceived a team player to be. They're very connected socially—not only through face-to-face interactions but through text messaging and e-mailing. They're very service oriented, they're excellent time managers, they're structured, and they're the most protected of any generation in U.S. history. There are more female, Asian, Hispanic, and immigrant students in this particular generation than in any generation to ever go to college—one in five are children of immigrants. They are video-game savvy, marking over 10,000 hours of screen time before their first day of college. There have been more technological innovations in the lifetimes of this particular generation than in any previous generation. Immediacy of response is very critical for this group. Seventy percent use instant messaging to keep in touch, 41 percent use e-mail to connect with teachers and classmates, and 81 percent use e-mail to stay in touch with friends and family (Moore 2007). As an example of the generation gap, I have a "millennial" daughter who communicates with me frequently via text messaging. When she text-messages me and I respond, it takes me several minutes to type out a simple "How are you doing?" Within seconds of sending

---

Dr. John E. Jacobson is Dean of the College of Education at Stephen F. Austin University in Nacogdoches, Texas.

the message, she replies with a couple of paragraphs. Her quickness in text messaging seems to be a characteristic of this generation; my slow response, a characteristic of my own.

With millennials' great acceptance and use of technology, it should come as no surprise that technology is greatly impacting education at both the K–12 and the higher education levels. Michigan will soon require K–12 students to experience online learning before graduating from high school. Last year Georgia passed a law allowing cyber charter schools. North Carolina created the North Carolina Virtual Public School, and Missouri passed a law to create a new state-led program that will include both full-time and part-time students in grades K–12. Thirty-eight states have e-learning initiatives, including virtual schools, cyber charter schools, online testing, or Internet-based professional development. Twenty-five states have statewide or state-led virtual schools. In 2000, there were 40,000 to 50,000 enrollments in K–12 online education. In 2002–2003, there were 328,000 distance education enrollments in K–12 public school districts (the most recent year data are available). The Peak Group has estimated that online enrollments in 2005 were at 500,000 (State Legislatures 2007).

Just as e-learning has expanded in K–12 schools, so has it in higher education. According to Andrea Foster and Dan Carnevale (2007), the number of students who exclusively take online courses has grown from 194,580 in 2000 to 1,518,750 in 2006 (see fig. 1). And about 3.2 million students took at least one online course during the fall of 2005—up 39 percent (2.3 million) from the previous year.

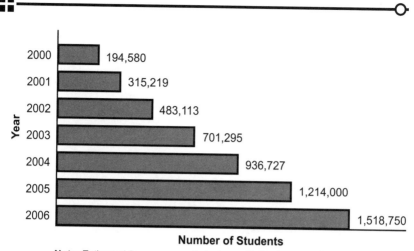

Year	Number of Students
2000	194,580
2001	315,219
2002	483,113
2003	701,295
2004	936,727
2005	1,214,000
2006	1,518,750

Number of Students

Note: Estimated figures cover students enrolled at U.S. degree-granting institutions that provide financial aid under Title IV.

Source: Eduventures

Figure 1. Number of Students Who Enroll Only Online. *(Chronicle of Higher Education* 53 [34]: A49.)

Currently, the most popular outlet for online delivery is the University of Phoenix. It has the lion's share, but in the next couple of years the major universities will be equipped to compete and take some of that share for themselves.

Stephen F. Austin State University (SFASU) mirrors U.S. universities in online delivery growth (see fig. 2). In particular, the College of Education at SFASU has become a big leader in online program development and offerings, having far more online programs in 2007 than it did in 2000. SFASU has an enrollment of about 11,500 students, 3,400 of which are in the College of Education, which makes up about 30 percent of the university. SFASU is rurally located in deep East Texas, about 2.5 hours northeast of Houston. If it is to grow its graduate enrollment, it must occur through an online delivery system.

In 2000, SFASU began offering its first online programs, with an online post-baccalaureate program for initial teacher certification at the elementary and secondary levels. In these programs, students may apply up to eighteen hours of their course work toward a master's degree. These initial online programs were immediately successful. Since then, SFASU has developed and now offers full master's degrees in Educational Leadership, Early Childhood Specialist, Standard Elementary, Content Emphasis, Music Education, and Resource Interpretation. It has also expanded into offering certifications in Family and Consumer Sciences, ESL and Bilingual Education, Master Reading, and Reading Specialist, and is working on an international teaching certificate to be delivered worldwide. Undergraduate online programming has been more challenging, but recently two new baccalaureate degrees have been added: a bachelor degree that allows nurses to move from RN to BSN, and a Bachelor of Science in Interdisciplinary Studies with Early Childhood Through Fourth Grade (EC-4) Teacher Certification Completer Program.

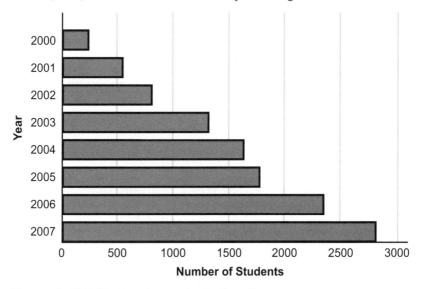

Figure 2. SFASU Enrollment in Online Courses.

With online programming beginning to flourish nationwide, skeptics have begun questioning online program quality. It's one thing to develop a series of PowerPoint presentations and put them into a WebCT type shell and call it an online course, but quite another to put into place and maintain a quality assurance system for online program delivery. SFASU has established the Office of Instructional Technology to oversee distance education. Policies were developed to govern course development, ownership, faculty compensation, and course and program quality. At SFASU, individual courses may be approved, but the development of full programs is given preference. To offer online courses at SFASU and receive an additional stipend for teaching an online course, faculty members are required to successfully complete a thirty-four-hour training program. The course approval process is rigorous, requiring demonstration of good teaching principles and several levels of approval. Students are charged a $25 fee per each credit hour of an online course. This fee is used to pay faculty a $2,500 course development fee and a $1,000 stipend each time a course is taught. All courses are evaluated each semester by students, and online courses are reviewed regularly to ensure course and program relevance and quality.

Recently the College of Education at SFASU has sought several outside grant sources—many of them through the U.S. Department of Education—to help with the development of online programming. Some of these grants are listed below.

- Early Intervention Training Program (Project Vision), U.S. Dept. of Education: $1.5 million is used to train visually impaired teachers living in four northwestern states via distance education.

- Consortium for Excellence in Rural Teacher Preparation (CERT-Prep), U.S. Dept. of Education: $2.1 million is used to identify and prepare teachers living in twenty-five rural school districts.

- Consortium for Excellence in Rural Teacher Preparation (CERT-Prep)—ELL, U.S. Dept. of Education: $1.5 million is used to identify and prepare teachers living in seven rural school districts and help SFASU make modifications to the online curriculum that enhance teachers' skills in English language learning.

- Developing Entrepreneurial Vision for Exemplary Leadership and Ongoing Professionalism (Project Develop), U.S. Dept. of Education: $820,000 helps SFASU and its twenty-one school-district partners identify, prepare, and support future principals.

Another of these grants is from the Fund for the Improvement of Postsecondary Education (FIPSE). This $600,000 grant has helped SFASU enhance its EC–4 Completer Program, which is designed to help paraprofessionals earn a bachelor's degree with Texas EC–4 teacher certification. We have found that many paraprofessionals in Texas want to become teachers—and would make excellent teachers—but they can't quit their jobs to go to school due to personal reasons (single parent raising children, live too far from a university). Whatever the obstacle, this grant helps paraprofessionals overcome the barriers to earning a degree and teacher certification through distance education. SFASU has joined with twenty-two Texas community colleges—representing approximately 45 percent of all community college students—to recruit, mentor, and support paraprofessionals in their goal to become teachers. The first two years of student learning are offered through the community college (many offer online and face-to-face options), and then students transfer into SFASU's two-year EC–4 Completer Program. Paraprofessionals can continue to work in the schools where they are employed and take all course work online. At this time, SFASU requires participants to come to campus once a semester for a two-day seminar, where they will meet with teachers and observe teaching in the nationally accredited Early Childhood Laboratory and the Texas-exemplary-rated Charter Campus School.

In this online program, SFASU provides university faculty mentors, chats, video clips of best teaching strategies, and other activities. Teacher work samples that demonstrate student learning, lesson design, and so forth are required. If paraprofessionals qualify for the Texas Aide Exemption, student teaching is waived and all field experiences are embedded in their regular course work. Observation evaluation has typically been through students video-taping and sending their captured lessons to professors for critique and grading. Under this model, by the time students receive the feedback, the "teaching moment" is lost. Thanks to the FIPSE grant, SFASU has purchased laptop computers and Webcams so that observation can take place in real time, along with pre-observation and post-observation capabilities. After much research, SFASU selected a product called Elluminate for its Webcam observation tool (www.elluminate.com). This videoconferencing tool allows for secure transmission between parties using a link sent through e-mail for connecting to a meeting and easily punches holes through school district firewalls.

Graduates of the EC–4 Completer Program have experienced much success, achieving a 100 percent pass rate on the mandatory state teacher certification exams. The program is recognized through the National Council for the Accreditation of Teacher Education. Graduates in May 2007 were largely diverse in terms of age and ethnicity. Several have reported that if it weren't for this online program, they would not have been able to complete a four-year degree and become teacher certified. Preparing paraprofessionals to become teachers is significant. With the great demand for teachers and the struggle to retain good teachers, SFASU has found that paraprofessionals who become teachers are more likely to stay in their communities and remain in the profession.

I began this brief paper by describing the characteristics of students who now make up our college classrooms—the millennials. Because of the nature of these students, online degree and certification programs are becoming increasingly popular. As most universities are experiencing, SFASU's online courses fill up first. As we develop online offerings, attention to quality and program delivery is critical. Finding viable quality alternatives to traditional face-to-face modes of instruction is imperative. The use of Webcams, online chats and blogs, streaming video, text messaging, and other technologies holds great promise in meeting the needs of today's students.

References

Foster, Andrea, and Dan Carnevale. 2007. Distance education goes public. *Chronicle of Higher Education* 53 (34): A49.

Moore, Alicia. 2007. They've never taken a swim and thought about jaws: Understanding the millennial generation. *College and University Journal* 82 (4): 41–48.

State Legislatures. 2007. Trends and transitions: E-learning is everywhere. July/August.

⬤ ⬤ ⬤ Technology and Learning Within the Future Context of Global Sustainability Education

Glenn Thomas

This paper is intended to provide an overview of future global trends and issues that can inform pre-K–12 instruction and the corresponding teacher preparation programs designed to support best teaching practice. These comments are centered on two of the increasingly accelerating and profoundly influential areas of the emerging future of mankind: (1) technologies, and (2) climate change. Both of these areas are drivers of global interdependence as reflected by increasingly interconnected communications, economies, political concerns, environmental opportunities, human rights, knowledge development, and health rights within the "spaceship earth" metaphor. Either humankind will create and embrace the opportunities to use technology and social learning to conquer the common foe of global warming, or our children and grandchildren worldwide will suffer the catastrophic results. The real question is, Are our schools that prepare today's children—the technologies that support them and the social structures that foster their ethics—forward-looking and comprehensive enough to meet the emerging challenges for the world citizens of 2030 and beyond?

The genesis of this paper was a conversation conducted a few months ago at the United Nations, where I was a delegate from one of 143 countries gathered not only to discuss concerns for today's children, but to project those concerns into their emergence as adults in an environment that will be vastly different from today's. Our discussions over several days revolved around the need to link sustainability, education, and technologies in ways that transcend boundaries of knowledge, location, language, gender, race, nationality, culture, and politics.

I want to use sustainability as an example of how we impart teaching-learning through the use of technology, looking at the creative and social implications, and then project to the year 2030 and ask, What are the

Glenn Thomas is Executive Director of PK–12 Schools and Programs, College of Education at Florida Atlantic University in Boca Raton, Florida. He is responsible for several university research schools in multiple locations, an environmental education center/graduate program and a large-scale innovative teacher development program.

implications for educators in terms of what we teach children, how we teach children, and what they should be able to know and do as they develop over a lifetime into increasingly informed and active global citizens? It is also important to note that several important fostered human characteristics that are essential for the future are not represented in this discussion, notably creativity development.

The Millennium Project's Report

The Millennium report, commissioned by the United Nations, asked 213 experts from across the globe to look ahead to 2030 and describe what they see in terms of future technologies and learning support for all kinds of people—not just educators but businesspeople, families, retirees, and others. The challenge elicited nineteen basic possibilities, which were assigned a probability and ultimately sorted, resulting in the following fifteen important projected influences for the future of learning:

Future Technologies

Just-in-time knowledge and learning

Individualized education

E-teaching

Broadened use of simulation

Web 17.0

Integrated lifelong learning systems

Global online simulations as a primary social science research tool

Portable artificial intelligence devices

Smarter-than-human computers

Use of public communications to reinforce pursuit of knowledge

Brain Enhancement

National programs for improving collective intelligence

Chemistry for brain enhancement

Genetically increased intelligence

Keeping adult brains healthier longer

Other Influences

Improved individualized nutrition

Of the nineteen possibilities, only four are perceived to have a less than 50 percent chance of occurring:

Hate and prejudice prevention programs

Continuous evaluation of human learning systems

Mapping of human synapses

Artificial microbes enhanced intelligence

The first of these is just-in-time knowledge and learning—acquiring knowledge and skills as they are needed. This idea is really interesting because it's not a single human being acting in isolation but within an expanding and increasing specialized global learning community, which is in constant formation and destruction as learners migrate from learning area to learning area, driven by motivation and supported by technology to bridge experience, educational level, distance, time, and preferred media/modality. It involves employing such tools as nanotechnologies, global positioning satellites, infrared cameras, and smart instrumentation to gather and catalog a vast array of information. It leverages the collective cognition of humanity to help make not just discipline-based (engineering, economic, chemical, social) decisions, not just locale (city, state, national, regional) decisions, but integrated interdisciplinary and perhaps ethical decisions from a global perspective. In such a context, how much could a student "memorize" in a knowledge-exploding subject such as biogenetics? Given that all the knowledge that has been developed from the beginning of man's history until today in the field of biogenetics will be doubled in the next four months, the challenge is apparent. Clearly in a global environment with the latest technology at our fingertips, just-in-time learning is an answer. Teachers today may initiate technology-supported projects in their classrooms as a way to see how students synthesize ideas, employ basic skills in creative ways, and connect processes to generate broader solutions. In these scenarios, students learn how to manipulate fractions only when they need to know how to manipulate fractions to solve an interdisciplinary, real-life simulated problem—not when that operation is the subject of the next math chapter.

A second major influence involves individualized education, which often incorporates technology from birth through death—including, for example, intergenerational learning opportunities. One of the emerging opportunities for youngsters is connecting their technology expertise to senior citizens who need to know how to send e-mail, edit pictures, create searches, explore virtual museums, project voice over IP, and perform other just-in-time tasks that inform and enrich. In a sense, this is e-learning, but it takes place face-to-face initially and then constructs new learning at a distance and across time.

Another important influence is the broader use of simulations. Today we use programmable mannequins in the medical community, and they can simulate any kind of illness, such as a disease that a doctor might only see once or twice during his or her entire practice. Blood pressure, body temperature, and a host of other variables can be induced through technology. Students can postulate causes, attempt remedies, and perhaps even "kill" the patent, inducing powerful learning experiences with no harm done. Simulations may also integrate very complex and progressive scenarios. For example, the effects of national policy options could be simulated by policy variable, to predict the effect of each option on other nations, on poverty, on disease, or even on climate change.

Integrated lifelong learning systems, which refers to a kind of artificial intelligence behind technology-supported learning systems, is another interesting predicted influence. These systems "learn and store" what an individual likes to learn, how he or she prefers to have learning stimulated, and how best to make those most current things and processes individually accessible. The implication is that assessment by an integrated learning system happens continuously, as a natural part of the stream of learning, rather than being artificially administered at designated points in time along the way, and that with each student action not only is the student assessed, but the system adds information and becomes "smarter" about the student's learning modalities, concept mastery, application, and so on. With this system, students are continuously learning, with assessment focused on improving the individual's learning process and learning goals rather than on attaching a grade to each student. That's really the way our children learn best. This will be increasingly possible with more precise artificial intelligence, improved global online simulation, and exploding content across a variety of media.

Accessing the Global Community

It is not easy to predict the future or foster the change necessary to successfully meet future challenges. Uncertainty can create fear and immobility or it can create new opportunities to be seized. This is certainly true of learning models, technology applications, and climate-change projections. In the scientific community, truth comes from replicability. If someone can replicate what someone else did and get the same results over and over, that's important, but even then, scientists would not say the concept is "true"; just that it's a more valid theory. In the public sector, innovation in policy and use of resources is not driven by best scientific theory (although that might be often preferable); it is driven by perceived trust in public officials. Given the status of public trust, projections of the future and extension of innovations will require increasingly more complex modeling, better use of technologies, and more transparency for public learning and political mobilization.

There are huge economic, educational, environmental, and ethical climate-change opportunities for future-oriented organizations and individuals. Technology must continue to evolve as a learning, informational, and interpersonal support tool. Florida's students today have traditional virtual learning opportunities, but many experiential learning opportunities remain bound in place, time, and presentation mode. Environmental centers/exhibits/museums, alternative energy sites, various ecosystems, green buildings, green policy discussions, and similar venues can provide rich experiential learning opportunities but are not accessible to the 2.7 million other students around Florida. Technologies can improve accessibility.

In terms of creative and social influences and the future implications for educators, the human focus shifts from decisions bound in time, resources, data, and space to streamed, uniquely situational decisions. In other words, a general direction for a decision becomes increasingly focused and may be ethically adjusted as more information is gathered. The effect of potential decisions on the front end can be simulated and communicated, so that decisions can be analyzed and adjusted based on real-time, emerging information as they are implemented. This concept of in-stream decision making is another interesting future component when viewing the role and purpose of global technologies for students.

In twenty-three years, our kindergartners will be deeply interconnected. As successful citizens, they will use a collective knowledge rather than only personal knowledge to make business and personal decisions. Citizens will be able and expected to participate in a rapid systemic global response to issues through technologies. They will immediately know details about an event across the globe: they'll know why from multiple perspectives; they'll view and evaluate the effect; they'll understand and perhaps participate in response; and they'll be able to see, communicate (virtual language translation), and support the people involved. There are also major implications for government and business ethics. Today governments, corporations, organizations, and individuals perpetuate injustice around the world. The collective will of future citizens armed with increased awareness and connectivity of broadened technological environments will make continuance of such injustice much more difficult. In a world that today spends $20 billion in bribes, imagine how those funds could be repurposed in the future to support education, environment, health, and other socially beneficial initiatives.

Technology has the potential to bridge emotive communication, which can improve cooperation. Body language, voice inflection, and eye position help us interpret what a person is really saying, and a Webcam can certainly assist with that. Being able to share emotions with others thousands of miles away will do a lot to foster trust, which is absolutely essential for citizens to act collaboratively about climate, conflict, economic disparity, and other issues in a global political environment.

The Future Is Green

So how future-ready is Florida? With about 3,600 public schools and another 1,700 private schools, the state houses about 210,000 total classrooms, but no "green school." Palm Beach County Schools—in partnership with Florida Atlantic University, College of Education, Pine Jog Environmental Center—is constructing Florida's first "green" elementary school and adjacent university environmental education center within a 135-acre outdoor classroom. The environmental education center is the primary site for visiting schoolchildren and the public, environmental education graduate program delivery, teacher development and in-service, curriculum development, grant and contract efforts, exhibits and community events, property stewardship and interpretative trail support, staff and researcher work spaces, after-school program and activity support, and classroom and lab space. Students of all ages can study the natural and built environments within the context of sustainability. Elementary and university students, school and university faculty, researchers, and the public will have access to the school, the environmental center, and the natural features of the outdoor site either on-site or at a distance via Webcams, external wireless instrumentation, alternative energy system performance data (solar hot water, photovoltaics), rainwater harvesting measurement/calculations, building and natural site electronic sensors, integrated energy monitoring systems, electronic data reports, and graphic displays. A creative model curriculum is being collaboratively developed, which incorporates the front edge of sustainability as well as Florida's performance standards in an interdisciplinary way. For example, individual and group projects reflecting the state standards from several disciplines— themed around local and global sustainability issues, and employing the various technologies—will serve as a platform for developing more independent and engaged lifelong learners.

Students entering the front door will see a wide variety of instrumentation through large windows, solar panels on the roof, and cold-water air-conditioning chiller towers. In their classes, instead of completing the odd-numbered problems in the back of their math book, these students will be pulling up spreadsheets of building performance data or rain collection and working from that—some from the previous day; some from the previous week. They will be looking at similar structures in non-green schools or buildings to compare, analyze, model, project, and draw inferences from data that are actual and real time—products of technology as opposed to artificial problems or pretend data from "the book." These students will have the interdisciplinary opportunities to apply green principles, supporting technologies, communication tools, and higher-order thinking skills not only within the local context of West Palm Beach, Florida, but—just as importantly—to the world community.

Conclusion

The bottom line is that there are very bright opportunities for important and active connections between lifelong learning, emerging technologies, and global climate-change challenges. We have an opportunity as educators to prepare our children to drive the changes they wish to see—in both the world in which they will live and the future they will pass along to their children. Our children will inherit "spaceship earth" in concert with children across the world, and all need to be equipped to address in an informed, ethical, creative, and collaborative manner the issues of life quality in a flattened and interdependent global community.

References

Barzilai, S., and A. Zohar. 2008. Is information acquisition still important in the information age? *Education and Information Technologies* 13 (1): 35–53.

De Bono, E. 2006. Technology and Creativity: As technology advances there's a layer of concept design being overlooked. http://www.thinkingmanagers.com/management/technology-creativity.php.

Fluck, E. A. 2001. Social effects of new technology in education. *Journal of Information Technology Impact* 2 (2): 43–54.

Glenn, J. C., and T. J. Gordon. 2007. *State of the future.* Washington, DC: Millennium Project, World Federation of UN Associations.

Kanuer, K., ed. 2007. Global warming: The causes, the perils, the solutions, the actions: What you can do. TIME, Inc. Special Publications. www.time.com/time/specials/2007/environment.

May, G. H. 1996. The social implications of information technology. *Inventing the Future: Partnerships for Tomorrow*, January. Available from www.partnerships.org.uk/itf/socimp.html.

Rieck, D. 2006. How technology changed creativity. *DMNews*, February 17.

Schomberg, R. 2007. From the ethics of technology towards an ethics of knowledge policy and knowledge assessment. In *IFIP International Federation for Information Processing*. Boston: Springer.

Scoter, Van J., D. Ellis, and J. Railsback. 2001. Technology in early childhood education: Finding the balance. Northwest Regional Educational Laboratory. http://www.nwrel.org/request/june01/child.html.

Tung, W. F., and S. Y. Deng. 2006. Designing social presence in e-learning environments: Testing the effect of interactivity on children. *Interactive Learning Environments* 14 (3): 251–64.

UNESCO Education Sector. 2005. *Guidelines and recommendations for reorienting teacher education to address sustainability.* http://unesdoc.unesco.org/images/0014/001433/143370e.pdf.

⬤ ⬤ ⬤ But Can You Make IT Do This? Reshaping Our Business and Our Technology

Rick Eiserman

Rather than focusing on the application of technology to deliver instruction to students, I would like to consider the value of technology in a different way, namely by asking how states can use technology—as well as our operating procedures (business rules) and business partners—to capture data on teacher preparation and certification, and then use that data to view student achievement and school improvement.

Over the last fifteen to twenty years there have been a number of efforts by states to buy or build certification "systems." Many of those early efforts failed for a variety of reasons—the technology was not ready, the states themselves were not ready, or a little bit of both. The common denominator was the intent to automate and speed up the certification process, make information more available to customers, and capture enough data to document the process. The electronic scanning of such documents as college transcripts and application forms made a great amount of information readily available in an individual file, but not necessarily available as data that could be searched, compiled, and analyzed by pushing a few buttons.

When most people think of educator certification in their state, they still view the agency in charge of the process as the bad guys. We are the barriers; we are the obstacles; we are the bureaucratic red tape that keeps good teachers out of the classroom, as in "Oh, she would be such a wonderful teacher if she could just pass that content assessment." We must change not only that perception but also the actual process. Technology is one of the ways we can do that. As that great educational philosopher Wayne Gretzky said when reflecting on his hockey game, "You miss one hundred percent of the shots you don't take." Although we certainly do not have all the answers in Georgia, we often follow the Gretzky philosophy to take a number of "shots" and, in so doing,

Rick Eiserman is Director of Policy and Communications for the Georgia Professional Standards Commission in Atlanta, Georgia.

have found things that work well for us. My intent in sharing some of our experiences is to stimulate thinking about perceptions and the process as we all try to enhance our existing certification systems and improve their value.

Georgia is one of about fifteen states with an autonomous Professional Standards Commission (GaPSC)—run outside the state department of education—which is responsible for educator preparation, certification, and discipline. We have about 1.6 million students in grades P–12 and about 135,000 certified educators employed in 181 public school districts. Our certification database contains records on 230,700 educators who currently hold valid Georgia certificates. In fact, each of those educators averages more than three certificate "fields," placing more than 794,645 valid certificates into the database. To put our certification workload into perspective, in fiscal year 2007 we completed a little over 185,000 certificate transactions (issuance, denials, renewals, add-ons, upgrades, NCLB modifications), with an average processing time of about one week.

History

The GaPSC was formed in 1991, before the World Wide Web was available to share information. All of our information was stored on a mainframe computer, controlled by a data center managed by another agency—in other words, our data was not really our own. We had computer terminals to access some information, but had few word processors and no networks for sharing information. We still had a few typewriters, but some PCs were appearing—although the Pentium processor was only talked about by techies. Like most states, we had paper- or microfilm-based retrieval systems with information stored on documents, not in databases. And this was just sixteen years ago!

Our "system" was driven by the U.S. Postal Service, when an eighteen-wheeler pulled up every morning and unloaded hundreds of pieces of mail from people applying or asking about the status of their applications. All of our pending files were on paper, and inevitably one of our evaluators would put a file in a desk drawer and then go on vacation, a clear signal that that teacher was about to call and inquire about his or her certification status. We expended too much time playing "who has the file" and "telephone tag" with busy teachers who could only call between classes or right after school. Of course most of them could not get through to our office, but they did manage to contact their legislator or the governor. Our processing time in 1991 was somewhere between four and eight months, especially between June and October.

That means if an educator applied in June, it could be February before that educator received a certificate or found out that he or she was not "certifiable"—and the school year would be half over.

In 1994 we initiated a request for proposal (RFP) for a certification system, but only one contractor bid on it, which by Georgia law nullified the RFP. That event pushed our agency to decide that if we could not buy a system, we would build it ourselves. We were very fortunate to hire—and keep—a couple of incredibly smart information technology (IT) guys.* Since then, we have had a fairly consistent in-house IT staff that works alongside the rest of us as part of our agency. When the system does not work, they feel the pressure from their peers to fix it.

Very quickly we created a starter network of some of the shared Word documents. Although we were still working at desks with paper spread out all over the place, we learned how to scan and image documents and moved away from our microfilm storage/retrieval system. We looked to the Web for ways to access information and, just as importantly, to share the information in a secure mode with our customers. We also took a hard look at our certification business rules and procedures because we did not want to automate all of the Band-Aid, crisis-management procedures we had adopted over the years. We basically stepped back and rewrote all of our certification rules to simplify and streamline procedures, and gained additional benefits from our automation efforts. Staff members were involved in the rewrite, and they helped design the processes focused on our new computer screens, which gave them ownership of the process. In 1998 we moved from a mainframe to our own servers, and we have not looked back.

Partnerships and Trust

In the course of these efforts, we also took a hard look at our customers and decided we wanted some of them to be actual partners in the process, which is why the idea of trust is a critical component of our system. In fact, we believe that trust and partnerships have been almost as important as the technology used to build the system. As an example, there are state certification offices that are not willing to allow anyone outside their agency to determine whether or not a transcript in an educator's application file is "official." These offices view such decisions as their responsibility. On the other hand, our experience has shown the value, efficiency, and benefits that come from entrusting other players with some of these tasks. Since the school systems are responsible for hiring

---

* Two individuals instrumental in the technical design and development of our systems are Chuck McCampbell and Tom Hall.

educators and are accountable for the overall success of their schools, we realized they must be part of the certification team. We figured we could, with minimal effort, train a few individuals from each system and provide them unique access and system codes so that they could, if necessary, be held accountable for each transaction. We were initially concerned that they might feel overburdened and view the partnering as them doing our work, but we were also confident that once they saw the big picture, they would see the benefits they would obtain.

What had initially been our processing work at the state level became our work with the school system partners. We began by automating the renewal process, now known as **A**utomatic **C**ertification **R**enewal **S**ystem (ACRES). School systems access a secure screen; enter a secret password and the certification identification number of their employee; and verify that renewal requirements such as course work and background checks have been completed, and that copies of all documents are maintained in the individual personnel folder at the school system. They push a button, and we print, fold, stuff the certificate in an envelope, and put it in the mail within twenty-four hours. For years, school personnel offices all over our state received thank-you notes from teachers because they received their renewed certificates so quickly. Imagine! Thank-you notes from teachers to certification offices! As our partners saw the increased value of their role, the mutual trust went up and our processing time went down. In 1996, a little over 72,000 certificates were issued, and during our peak time—June through October—it still took about three months. Five years later, with more technology, rule tweaking, and partnering, almost 79,500 certificates were completed with a processing time of about six weeks. Today our processing time averages about one week, with approximately 60 percent of the transactions actually completed overnight. An unanticipated benefit of the system is that our evaluator staff actually works from home four days a week, which makes them a lot happier and a lot more productive.

ExpressLane

About a year and a half ago we implemented our version of an "almost online system," which we call ExpressLane. When a school system partner wants to submit a certification transaction, it enters our secure Web portal with a secret password and enters the certification identification number. Our certification system searches the database to see what, if any, certificates that individual holds. If the individual is not yet certified, the only transaction option is to request an initial certificate. However, if the individual is already certified, then other options are available. The school system—now driven by the actual certification data and business rules from our system—determines what transaction to initiate and is informed of exactly what documents must be included in the application packet. A random number is automatically generated with instructions, and is faxed over a secure network back to the school system. The school system then obtains and arranges the required documents in the proper order and faxes the documents to our server. The random number on the cover sheet identifies the specific school system transaction and employee identification number; the computer converts the fax images into a TIF image; and the entire electronic packet is routed to an evaluator for processing. No paper is ever printed from the secure fax transaction. Since all required documents are present in a set sequence, most ExpressLane applications, which now constitute about 65 percent of our cases, are processed in a day.

Hi-Q

We have recently implemented what we call the Hi-Q (Highly Qualified) system, merging our certification database information with the state department of education employment database. As a result, central office personnel or school building principals in Georgia can access Hi-Q through our secure Web portal, which provides a list of all the teachers in the school or system, and indicates who is, and is not, highly qualified by our state's definition, and why. The administrator can click on any one of the individuals and see specific details, such as certificates held, tests passed, and teaching assignments. The system also identifies a variety of options that would make the educator highly qualified: reassign the teacher into subjects for which he or she is certified; pass a content assessment; complete some course work; and so on. The Hi-Q system enables administrators to keep track of Hi-Q percentages and status with the click of a button, and guides them through the process of putting together an individualized plan for those who are not yet highly qualified. Our partners readily see the value of Hi-Q and realize it only works when they help keep the certification and employment database records current.

Teacher Distribution

The equity in teacher distribution is an important piece of NCLB. Our technology, and the efforts of our partners, allowed us to design a database called EQUITY, which calculates such information as school building/district AYP status, student population by ethnicity, percent of free and reduced lunch, years of teaching experience, teacher turnover, and a variety of other factors that contribute to school improvement and student achievement. Local school administrators can access our secure portal and view data across schools—within their district as well as statewide. When we see individual schools not making AYP, we often see that a number of the teachers do not have many years of experience, and there is usually an accompanying high turnover rate. This is important information for those making decisions in schools, and it can now be accessed across the state.

What's Next?

Like other states, we now find ourselves at a critical stage in the ongoing refinement of our database system. As discussed, most certification systems were built to speed up processing and capture only enough data to document the transaction. If specific information is desired, such as the college program the teacher completed, that information can be found by going into the individual electronic record.

Certification officials are not normally interested in capturing (entering) a lot of data that is not going to streamline the process. But technology has matured, and the need for data analysis has changed in recent years. A great deal of data is now desired to enable researchers to analyze information on teacher quality, preparation, assessments, and other variables that have been previously unavailable. To certification officials, who tend to focus on processing, it sometimes seems that if it were up to the researchers, they would want someone to enter data on whether teachers have blue eyes or brown eyes. That way, future researchers could determine whether or not blue-eyed teachers have a greater impact on student achievement than brown-eyed teachers.

One of the next issues, then, is how to modify and enhance our current systems and procedures to collect more data for analysis without slowing down the processing time. There is no doubt that data is essential to improving student achievement and school improvement. There is also no doubt that certification officials and many other players must come to the table and address these issues of what and how much data to collect, and how it can be shared.

A great amount of assistance and informed guidance has been produced by the Data Quality Campaign. Its efforts to promote and support the development of statewide longitudinal databases that link both student and teacher data have benefited a number of states. Through its conferences and publications, which focus on the use of data as a flashlight to illuminate rather than a hammer to discipline, many states are making progress. But can you make IT do this...? We still have much hard work to do at the state level, but by reshaping our business, applying new technologies, and sharing lessons learned, we will get there.

⚫ ⚫ ⚫ Collecting Quality Data for Effective Decision Making

Dale Janssen

When it comes to teacher preparation programs, California is on the cutting edge, particularly in terms of innovations—High Tech High being one stand-out example. In terms of data collection, however, we are far behind.

According to the quick-witted Sherlock Holmes: "It's a capital mistake to theorize before one has data. Insensibly, one begins to twist facts to suit theories instead of theories to suit facts." Truer words on the subject have never been spoken; if you don't have good data, you aren't going to make good decisions.

Data is defined in the dictionary as "factual information used as a basis for reasoning, discussion, or calculation." While this seems very straightforward, it is important to consider the second definition as well: "information output by a sensing device...that includes both useful and irrelevant or redundant information." Data is only as good as the quality of the information going in. We need to be able to look at what we have collected and determine its value. According to Finagle's Third Law: "In any collection of data, the figure most obviously correct, beyond all need of checking, is the mistake." California is currently in the process of using data in two areas: (1) for professional preparation and program accreditation, and (2) for the creation of a statewide teacher data system.

The Accreditation System

The Commission on Teacher Credentialing—an independent standards board dedicated to ensuring both quality in terms of preparatory conduct, and professional growth of California's public school teachers—is in the process of developing a new accreditation system, and determining what types of data should be collected for that system. The data will then be used for program improvement as well as for accreditation purposes.

───○─

Dale Janssen is Executive Director for the Commission on Teacher Credentialing in Sacramento, California.

One of the data points that will most likely be collected is a Teacher Performance Assessment (TPA). The TPA—ready to be implemented in 2003, but stalled due to a budget crisis—will be a requirement for every teacher in California as of July 1, 2008. The advantage of the TPA is that it sets a statewide standard for assessing the performance of a teaching candidate.

CalTPA

The commission's TPA model is the California Teacher Performance Assessment (CalTPA), which is based on the thirteen Teacher Performance Expectations developed by both the commission and the Educational Testing Service. The CalTPA is just one of many forms of teacher preparation tools that institutions are going to be using to determine a candidate's qualifications for earning a teaching credential. There are currently fifteen institutions taking part in a CalTPA pilot study, and these institutions have been collecting data and turning it in to the commission since 2003. The CalTPA involves a series of four performance tasks, of which all but the first is done with actual K–12 students. The first task is the Subject-Specific Pedagogy, which asks the candidate to use scenarios created around hypothetical students to identify appropriate subject-specific instruction and assessment plans, and adapt this information to particular focus students. The second task is Designing Instruction, which requires a candidate to make appropriate connections between what he or she knows about individual students in the class and his or her instructional plans for those students. The third task is Assessing Learning, which requires a candidate to demonstrate his or her ability to design standards-based, appropriate student assessment activities in the context of the whole class and for particular focus students. In California, everything is standards based, and teacher preparation programs are aligned with K–12 content standards. The last task, Culminating Teaching Experience, ties everything together in that a candidate must design a standards-based lesson for a class of students and then teach that lesson to students within a classroom setting. This task, which essentially judges the candidates' student-teaching performance, is videotaped, both so that the candidate has an opportunity to self-reflect on the program and to assure reliability in scoring. Because of how these tasks are organized, universities submitting data for the Teacher Performance Assessment can clearly see how they're doing in light of the scores their candidates are receiving. If, for example, the data clearly shows a low score in task three—the assessment task—the university can put its efforts into making improvements in that area of teaching.

PACT

An alternative teaching performance assessment to the CalTPA is the Performance Assessment for California Teachers, or PACT, which was just recently approved by the commission. This assessment—based on an eight-point scale—is intended to improve the quality of teacher education, measure and promote equitable teaching practices, and strengthen teaching and student performance. When results show that there is a problem with some aspect of the scoring, the state knows it needs to go back and look at the assessment standard to make certain that it is appropriate. With this kind of data available, it is that much easier to make informed decisions.

Teacher Surveys

Another valuable source of data are first-year teacher surveys. There are three sets of surveys: one is a self-report, one comes from a principal, and one comes from a peer. The surveys include questions organized around six domains, which are aligned with the Teacher Performance Expectations. These surveys are based on a five-point scale, so it can be easily determined what areas still have room for improvement. Once again, this is another area of rich data that a program can use for its own improvement.

The California State University Model

Although the commission has not decided on specific data points yet, the California State University (CSU) system has had a model in place for evaluating teacher preparation programs since 2001. The CSU system collects data from first-year teaching graduates and their supervisors based on six outcomes, which I discuss below.

Outcome one is an exit evaluation by those who have completed their preparation program. This evaluation measures new teachers' views about their readiness to begin teaching and the adequacy of their preparation programs in several domains of the curriculum—that is, their views of completeness and satisfaction with the program. The exit evaluation is completed via a confidential online survey. Outcome two is an evaluation by those who have completed a program and have been teaching for one or more years. This outcome measures the value and effectiveness of preparation in practice, as teachers answer online surveys based on their own work-related experiences following their first and third years of teaching. Outcome three consists of evaluations by supervisors of first-year teachers. These supervisors are the individuals who assess a first-year teacher's performance and make decisions about whether to retain or drop that teacher before the second year. These online surveys are very similar to the ones being completed by first-year teachers for

Outcome two, which allows CSU to compare the answers of the two groups. Outcome four is the Teacher Performance Assessment, which will eventually consist of CalTPA and PACT assessment scores. CSU is currently using another series of assessments while making preparations for the implementation of a uniform TPA. Outcome five relates to participation and retention of teachers, which will eventually evaluate retention up to eight years. A recent analysis of those staying and those leaving constituted an evaluation of teacher preparation by measuring the extent to which preparation was cited as a contributing factor to career decisions. Last is Outcome six, which is probably the most difficult and definitely the most politically contentious in California, and I suspect in other states as well. Outcome six involves linking K–12 student achievement to the preparation of those students' teachers. Suitable evidence regarding this claim is difficult to come by. CSU is currently in the process of gathering evidence—including quantitative indicators of economic and demographic factors shown to affect learning—to be better able to evaluate campus programs.

The Teacher Longitudinal Data System

Unlike Georgia's success with uniting teacher and student data so that everything is in one place, when it comes to statewide data, California is extremely fractured. Teacher data currently resides in multiple databases at various state and local agencies with no mechanism for integration. Because we issue the credentials, the commission has all an individual's credential information saved in a database. The California Department of Education—a separate entity—collects demographic information about teachers and students, and has a rich database regarding where teachers are assigned. In just these two agencies alone there is a great deal of information overlap as well as a lack of quality data, resulting in inefficiency and a dearth of high-quality analysis.

In order to streamline the process of collection, storage, and analysis, California's embarking on a teacher database called the California Longitudinal Teacher Integrated Data Education System, or CALTIDES— an appropriate acronym for this coastal state. This system—currently at the request-for-proposal stage—is based on California's new CALPADS system, a data system that allows for the tracking of a student's academic performance over time. The same technology going into the student system will be used to develop the teacher system, which will result in savings of both time and money. All the assignment information will be done by computers versus by hand by the commission, which is currently responsible for looking at teacher assignments, and so will really enhance what we do in California. The CALTIDES is expected to be complete by 2010.

Conclusion

The Center for the Future of Teaching and Learning reports every two years on the status of the teaching profession in California. A recent report found that schools teaching grades one through three had the least experienced teachers. This report resulted in two pieces of legislation. The first—which passed despite the objections of the union—gives principals the authority to make decisions about assignments regardless of seniority. The second gives additional money and time to pre-service for interns focused on EL, to enrich the experience of those who tend to be focused on those grades.

Something I think we need to keep in mind always is the reliability of actual data versus anecdotal data, on which policy decisions are too often based. Perhaps we've heard ten people saying the same story, and so in our minds the details of the story become fact. However, it is extremely important for everyone to remember that anecdotal information is not reliable in the same way that verifiable data is.

In terms of teacher preparation, we've witnessed through the pilot study universities using the Teacher Performance Assessment to identify areas where they need to make program improvements. We at the commission also anticipate being able to make statewide decisions based on data presented to us. In the near future, data will play an important role in California.

O O O Educator Perspective and Learner Efficacy: The Promise of Technology in Education

W. Robert Houston

Education today is undergoing the most rapid, promising, and exciting revolution in the history of the human race. That revolution is fueled by electronic technology and globalization. For educators seeking more effective ways to prepare the younger generations for an unknown future, it represents our greatest challenge, for we must involve ourselves in techniques and processes that are unknown to us as well. We are beginning to see a glimmer of that future—the use of computers and PowerPoint rather than blackboards and chalk; the use of the Internet for seeking information rather than books; customized instruction based on technology; and the massive storage potential of electronic information that is accurately and readily retrievable.

But for all the changes in education today, we have yet to develop the full potential of the technological revolution in which individualization is enhanced by the learner using his or her unique exploration of knowledge and procedures. Every facet of our world is changing more rapidly than ever before. While making considerable progress, education continues to fall further behind technological and global conditions and innovations. While education may have never been on the cutting edge of innovation, the increasing rapidity of changes makes the disparity even more obvious.

To put this in perspective, consider changes during the past decade, as charter schools and alternative certification have shifted the landscape of educational institutions away from university-dominated teacher education and the public school dominance of K–12 education. Or, to provide greater perspective, think about the education of children one hundred years ago in Laura Ingalls Wilder's rural Minnesota school or sixty years ago, when states began requiring a bachelor's degree for basic

Dr. W. Robert Houston is John and Rebecca Moores Professor and Executive Director at the Institute for Urban Education at the University of Houston in Houston, Texas.

teacher certification; when the GI Bill of Rights encouraged thousands of returning servicemen to attend college; when universal education was America's goal; and when universities became the dominant trainer of teachers.

Compare this with the thousands of years of pre-history, when future generations were trained by example, as fathers taught their sons to hunt, fight, and raise crops, and mothers taught domestic skills to their daughters; or the hundreds of years during which tutors taught only the sons of wealthy families (Greece, Rome, Persia), and the Middle Ages when clerics learned to read and write primarily for religious reasons.

Textbooks emerged as the primary technology during the past century, and schools the logical locations for educating children and youth—schools were more efficient, books were located there, and teachers and students could easily be brought to their central locations. It was a time of the great experiment—universal education—combined with the Industrial Revolution, which resulted in major educational changes, yet even greater changes will occur in the coming decade.

The question for us today is: Are educators prepared to embrace educational changes resulting from innovative uses of technology that are only glimmers of reality?

Vision and Purpose of Technology

Following this thorough exploration of the uses of technology, I can think of no better way to maintain our focus on the basic purpose of education than through the quotation, "As you go through life and set your goals, keep your eye on the donut and not the hole." The allure of technology, its enormous potential, and its endemic problems often tend to mask its purpose in education—to enhance the education of learners.

A few weeks ago, I observed six women and six teenage girls in a restaurant. The women were sitting at one end of a long table, chattering away, laughing, and socializing. The other end of the table was very quiet—the six girls were text-messaging each other and their other friends; it was their way of communicating. Children and youth are more comfortable with technology and innovations than their parents and teachers. They listen to iPods, watch YouTube, post on MySpace, communicate by cell phone, surf the Web to buy shoes or to look up information rather than reading a book or an encyclopedia. They use laptop computers to design simulated communities, become avatars, or enter virtual worlds. They are as comfortable with electronic technology as their parents were with television and the automobile.

Effective education requires the interrelationship between technology and teachers. Striking examples have been described about how technology is used in instruction to do what it does best, leaving teachers free to do what they do best. The human touch provides opportunities for shared emotion, for building trust and friendship, for supporting emergent partnerships and communities, for emulating moral and ethical behavior, and for stimulation and motivation. While we focus today on the contributions of technology in education, we must not forget that the teacher is vital to enhanced education (and perhaps the teacher is even a form of technology).

As we explore technology in education, one caveat is in order. With members of the younger generation spending greater proportions of their time alone (interacting with a computer, watching a football game or DVD), schools provide a valuable service to society as they bring children and youth together. A cornerstone of inventions and innovations today is teamwork—groups of people working together to solve problems. While technology plays a major role in the implementation of ideas, the driving force is human relations. Throughout this book we've been given numerous examples of how electronic technology is intertwined with human interaction and collaboration.

Technology is beginning to change the educational environment, but this often happens too slowly. PowerPoint is a primary tool that draws on the same instructional model as lectures and chalkboards—only it is more sophisticated. Excel has enhanced our management of large data sets, including teacher certification; the Internet and cell phone, our communication tools; online and distance learning courses, our access; and Microsoft Word, our writing and spelling tools. But these are simply new and more sophisticated ways of putting into practice the same instructional and management approaches. Simulations and gaming have provided increasingly sophisticated problem-solving tools, primarily designed for recreational purposes. Technology, per se, is not a panacea; it provides increased power for teaching, but it will not replace the personal interaction of a quality teacher or the instructional ineptness of unqualified individuals.

Progress Through Technological Innovations

The papers contained here outline striking examples of technological innovations. As echoed in *Star Trek*, we in education need to "go where no one has gone before." What is needed are tools that draw on the power of technology as children and youth are educated for a yet unknown and rapidly changing world. More so than in any previous generation, our young people need to draw on the vast storehouse of technology to become effective problem solvers, able to focus on innovative solutions to persistent problems. In real life, problems do not present themselves as multiple-choice options, nor do they always have a clean, clear, precise answer. Glenn Thomas identified some technologies that will influence education in the coming decades: just-in-time knowledge and learning, individualized education, e-learning, broadened use of simulation, Web 17.0, integrated lifelong learning systems, and global online simulations as a primary social-science research tool. Yet even these may be too-conservative estimates of the future, for they represent continued rather than exponential changes.

We need to draw on the challenges and developments of some of the computer games that our young people play today as models for instruction. We need to involve children early in seeking answers to real-life questions. Children and youth need to have the opportunity to explore problems of their own choosing. Self-confidence builds when they are provided with opportunities to learn through projects and problems. High Tech High in San Diego uses this approach. For example, students use sophisticated instruments to explore DNA, which leads to developing an understanding of basic biology. They may need to represent a specific nation at a mock UN and must therefore understand many factors related to their country in order to successfully represent the country when voting on issues.

It is an inverted approach: using a real, interesting, and complex problem situation to motivate students to learn about the basic concepts and structure of a discipline. In the language of science, they are engaged in an *experiment* rather than a *demonstration*. Such an approach could be based on gaming theories, the avatar concept, simulations, data-analysis tools, or real-life problems to solve or issues to consider.

Such an approach results in two outcomes: first, instruction is customized, as individual students explore different problems while learning how to learn and apply their learning; and second, students become empowered (i.e., efficacy) by learning they can solve their own problems.

The Time for Action Is Now

These essays have stimulated us to consider a wide range of technology-based innovations and innovative practices. It is clear that we are motivated to improve our practice, not just through incremental changes but by giant leaps to be able to draw on the most recent innovations and embrace new ideas and technology. The time to begin the process is now.

Thirty years ago I heard a fable while in Persepolis, the ancient capital of Persia. This fable was told in ancient times, but it is relevant today as we embark on potential education-changing programs. It is the story of a lion who thought he was a goat. As a cub, he became lost and was raised by a herd of goats. He learned to live like a goat—to eat grass and to stay with the herd. One day he saw a majestic animal bounding across the plains. He felt a primordial instinct to be with the animal, but he turned and ran away with the goats. The moral of the fable, 2,500 years old, is this—for one brief instant, he had the opportunity to be what he was born to be, but he chose instead to be simply a member of the herd.

The message of the story for us is clear: if we as educators are to make the major changes in education that are possible because of technology, we must begin now. We can no longer be members of the herd; we must begin educating differently, to focus on learning rather than teaching, to consider the changing learning patterns of today's youth, to draw on innovations in learning and brain research and in technology, and to begin that journey now.

That is our challenge, and how we respond, our destiny.

Books Available

from

Evaluation Systems

After Student Standards: Alignment

The Assessment of Teaching: Selected Topics

Bias Issues in Test Development

Continuing Discussions in Teacher Certification Testing

Current Topics in Teacher Certification Testing

Education Reform Success Stories

Educational Technology for Teacher Preparation and Certification

From Policy to Practice

How to Find and Support Tomorrow's Teachers

The Induction Years: The Beginning Teacher

Linking Standards and Assessment

Performance Assessment in Teacher Certification Testing

Perspectives in Teacher Certification Testing

Program Issues in Teacher Certification Testing

The Role of Technology in Tomorrow's Schools

Teacher Certification Testing: Recent Perspectives

Teachers of the Future, Schools of the Future

Teacher Preparation Assessment: The Hows and Whys of New Standards

Teacher Recruitment and Retention

Teachers: Supply and Demand in an Age of Rising Standards

What Is a Qualified, Capable Teacher?

To request these books, please write or call:
Publications Office
Evaluation Systems
Pearson
P.O. Box 226, Amherst, MA 01004-0226
(413) 256-0444